UNDISCOVERED
Riches™
How to Find Your Hidden Wealth

Roel Sarmago, CFP®

Valorton

UNDISCOVERED RICHES™
© 2016 by Roel Sarmago. All rights reserved.

Published by Valorton Publishing.

No part of this book may be used or reproduced in any manner whatsoever without the prior written permission of 10-10-10 Publishing or Roel Sarmago, except in the case of brief quotations embodied in reviews.

For information about special discounts for bulk purchases, please contact Valorton Publishing at 1-888-398-8835 ext. 902.

159-4936 Yonge St.
Toronto, Ontario Canada
M2N 6S3

Printed in the United States of America.

Cover photo courtesy of Rojotography, www.rojotography.com.

Library and Archives Canada Cataloguing in Publications information is available.

ISBN: 978-0-9949049-1-1 (paperback)
ISBN: 978-0-9949049-0-4 (ebook)

For Sonia,
Greggy and Bianca.
You are my WHY.

ACKNOWLEDGEMENTS

An amazing group of real-world real estate investors and active financial markets traders have influenced me directly and have indirectly influenced the creation of *Undiscovered Riches*™. I would especially like to thank my first real estate investing mentor and trainer, Pip Stehlik, for inspiring Sonia and I to take action towards living the life we truly wanted to live.

Along the way, many formal and informal conversations I've had with the following group of people have been instrumental in my understanding of the solutions to these money myths: Peter Massihi, Ross Lightle, Jean Lebeau, Shelley Hagen, Ronny Bukovsky, Rae Ostrander, Andy Tanner, Matt Justice, Noah Davidson and Sam Moussa.

It was Jeff English that gave me my start in financial services and Bill Jack that mentored me into an award-winning division director.

Thousands of clients, workshop participants and my own mentor students have helped me validate and fine-tune these concepts.

Direct influencers of this book include the good people at the Aaron Group and 10-10-10 Publishing, my editor George Verongos for turning my manuscript into a book and Shie-Mee Yeh for being the very first person to give me feedback on my rough draft.

Foreword

It is an honour and a privilege to write the foreword for Roel Sarmago's first book, *Undiscovered Riches*™. I know that Roel has wanted to write this book for over four years, since he left the world of mutual fund sales and it has been just over a year since he began writing this book in earnest.

I often teach my coaching clients that the quality of their answers depends on the quality of their questions. *Undiscovered Riches*™ is unique in that it answers many high quality questions about money and personal finances that you might not have even thought to ask, such as "What is the highest and best use of my money?" and "How can I generate more money more efficiently and more sustainably without sacrificing too much family time?" and "What fundamental assumptions about personal finances do I have that are keeping me from living my life to the fullest?"

Wow. These are big, important questions—the answers to which can be found within this book along with answers to other big important questions that will challenge you to see your financial life as it truly is.

As an accomplished real estate investor, success and investment coach, and author of several books on these topics myself over the past 40 years, I am impressed by Roel's keen observations about the world of money, investing and personal finances. Never before has anyone so clearly and concisely pointed out these seven money myths that have been deceptively holding people back for generations.

Roel Sarmago is the only Certified Financial Planner that I know of who specializes in financial coaching *outside* of the world of mutual funds and focuses on real estate and businesses with a sprinkling of active trading in the financial markets. So, you can imagine how his perspectives would differ quite a bit from the majority of run-of-the-mill traditional personal finance books that currently plague the market.

Undiscovered Riches™ is written in a fresh and sometimes cheeky voice that brings a welcome bit of levity to the typically dry, yet critically important, topic of personal finances and investing. The lighter side of Roel's writing is an integral part of the *Undiscovered Riches*™ reading experience, because it balances the gravity of the book's more serious facts, figures and warnings.

I invite you to snap out of the trance-like state that the media and your daily routine has kept you in, long enough to truly digest the wisdom contained within these pages. You'll thank me that you did.

You have made a good decision to read this book and it will serve you well to heed its important messages and apply them to your own life… before it's too late.

Raymond Aaron
"New York Times" Top-10 Bestselling
Coauthor, *Chicken Soup for the Canadian Soul*
Author, *Double Your Income Doing What You Love*

Table of Contents

Acknowledgments	v
Foreword	vii
Introduction	1
Myth #1: The Time is Money Myth	15
Myth #2: The Saving (and *Savings*) Myth	27
Myth #3: The Budgeting Myth	41
Myth #4: The Debt Myth	51
Myth #5: The Retirement Myth	65
Myth #6: The Net Worth Myth	79
Myth #7: The Home Equity Myth	87
Bonus Myth: The Diversification Myth	97
Putting it all Together	105
Afterword	117
About the Author	125

Introduction

Money can't buy everything...
but then again, neither can no money.

It was through a handful of casual conversations, like the one following, which inspired the creation of this book:

"So, are you a friend of the bride or the groom?" I said with a smile.

The well-dressed couple was sitting alone at the luxuriously prepared round table set for eight guests.

"The groom. And you?" said the gentleman.

"Same," I said as I found my name card to the man's left amongst the sparkling stemware and silverware. I was relieved to find out I was seated facing towards the presidential table.

"Cool. I'm Mike. This is my wife, Jenny," Mike said as he half-stood up shaking my hand motioning to his right with his other hand.

"Nice to meet you," Jenny said extending her hand without getting up, forcing me to reach across Mike.

"Nice to meet you too. My name's Roel. Roel Sarmago," I told the couple as I sat down.

"So, how do you know Alfredo?" Mike asked.

"Alfredo and Karen were my clients for several years."

"Oh, so you must be their financial planner. Alfredo mentioned we'd be sitting with you." Mike said.

"We already have insurance and our investments are doing pretty good right now." Jenny said a little curtly with a warm smile that didn't match her tone.

"Jenny!" Mike said in a hushed tone, a little embarrassed.

"No worries. I said they *were* my clients. I'm actually not in the industry anymore." I reassured the couple. They looked to be in their mid-thirties, late-thirties at most.

"Oh, yeah? So, what do you do now, Roel?" Mike asked.

"Pretty much I just manage my small real estate portfolio and I'm toying with the idea of writing a book." I said.

"Neat. What's your book about?" Jenny said, warming up a bit.

"Well, I don't want to seem like I'm trying to sell you anything," I said, as I gave Mike a wink that Jenny could obviously see.

"No, seriously," Jenny said. "I know you're not trying to sell us anything, so it's cool."

"She doesn't mince words, eh?" I said to Mike.

"Seriously," Mike said with a straight face.

Answering Jenny's question, I began, "Well, you know how a lot of people struggle with saving their money and paying down their debts?"

"Yeah," Mike and Jenny said in unison.

"And you know how relatively few people actually don't find it that hard to save money or pay off their credit cards every month?" I continued.

"Like us!" Jenny chimed in. "I read 'The Richest Man in Babylon' a few years ago and we've worked our way up to saving ten percent of every pay cheque," Jenny said proudly. "We've been doing that for a few years now. And we never keep a balance on our credit cards and we've accelerated our mortgage payments."

Mike gently nudged Jenny with his arm. Jenny gave the side of Mike's head an annoyed look with a curl of her upper lip and then turned her attention back to me.

"Right, so my book is for people in the second category—people like you, I guess—that already have a good grasp of the basics that conventional advice dictates, but are still wondering if there's a better more efficient way to manage their finances other than merely saving more or paying down debt faster."

"So, what's the answer?" Jenny jumped back in.

"You'll have to excuse my wife," Mike said with a laugh as he teased Jenny.

"What do you mean 'what's the answer?'" I asked Jenny.

"The answer. The next level. That's what you're getting at, right? What more can people like us do?" Jenny asked somewhat impatiently.

"That's a good question," I said. "I'm still working on how to articulate that. This might sound a bit philosophical, but basically, you know how the people in the first category—the ones that are still trying to grasp the basics of saving money and paying down debt—are in a sense trying to stop the flow of money?"

"By 'stopping the flow of money,' do you mean '*saving*' and '*holding*' for the long term?" Jenny asked.

"Exactly." I replied.

"Then, yes, that's like us." Jenny said hurriedly leaning in a bit. "Go on."

It was Mike's turn to give Jenny an annoyed look, which Jenny dismissed with a wave of her hand without looking at him.

"Well, ironically the 'answer,' as you put it Jenny, is once you have a good enough grasp of the basics is to actually look for more and better ways to get your money to *move* rather than continue to look for ways to slow it down or stop its flow altogether." I explained.

"What do you mean?" Mike and Jenny said in unison without missing a beat. I could tell they'd been married several years.

"What I mean is people should manage their financial lives like they're running a business. In business terms, rather than try to build up retained earnings, effectively *stopping* the flow or movement of money, the success of a business depends on increasing and diversifying income—*increasing* the flow or movement of money—and managing that income ever more *efficiently*. Stopping the flow of money would mean death for a business. So why should it be any different for individuals like you and me?"

"That's true! I never thought of it that way," Jenny interjected. "I'm a marketing channel manager at work and my boss is always saying 'you gotta manage your cash flow,

Jenny.' It's never about building up the company's cash reserves per se, although that's always a nice by-product, but making sure that we're always cash flow positive. If ever we have a cash surplus, I have to look for ways to re-deploy that cash to generate more income. And even if I have a lot of cash, but I'm not moving any inventory, I'm basically dead in the water."

"Exactly," I said, encouragingly.

"You know, that's really interesting, Roel." Mike added. "I went into business for myself a few years ago and only recently I've started to realize I don't actually like sitting on cash. A small amount is good, plus I have a business line of credit, so in case of emergency I'm fine. But I find myself constantly looking for ways to reinvest that cash in my business to generate more sales."

Mike put his arm around Jenny's shoulders. "To be honest, Jenny's an amazing saver. She's the one that's been maxing out our retirement contributions every year and managing our household budget. And, although I do take out a moderate salary for myself, everything else I earn is reinvested in the business to generate more sales. The best is when I've invested the time and money for the type of contract that will produce recurring orders over the following several months. When I have a few contracts like those all at the same time life is great!" Leaning towards me, Mike lowered his voice. "I actually realized that sitting on *too* much cash in my business does me no good." Leaning back again, Mike returned to his normal speaking voice and added, "I just never thought to apply the same principles to our personal finances."

Mike paused and looked away as he began connecting the dots. "So, you're saying that if we want to move beyond the basics, and in essence make life easier, we need to treat our personal finances like a business and, like a business, keep only a small amount of cash reserves—maybe add to that an emergency line of credit—and focus on activities that will get money to flow to us more efficiently and from multiple sources?"

"That's basically it. You got it." I said, proudly.

Unaffected by my encouragement, Mike continued his train of thought, "And by doing so, if I can get so efficient with generating cash flow that it requires less and less input of my personal time, then I really wouldn't ever have the need to retire, because the cash flow—like my multiple-order contracts—would continue to come in as if on auto-pilot."

"You catch on quick, Mike."

"OR..." Jenny jumped in. "We wouldn't have to wait until we're sixty-five in order to retire! What's to stop us from retiring ridiculously early once most, if not all, of our income is on auto-pilot?"

"Hey, whatever makes you happiest." I commented feeling a little like I'm being left out of the conversation.

"But how do we do all that?" Mike and Jenny said in unison, once again as they turned their attention back to me.

"Ah. For that, you'll have to wait until I've finished the book!" I said playfully.

Sustainable **financial freedom**

There are a number of insidious and pervasive myths going around that subconsciously have us believe that the answer to our personal financial dreams (or cause of our personal financial woes, depending on your angle) is the accumulation of a high, or "high enough," net worth. And, has us believe that the best way to acquire a high net worth is through the lifelong laborious setting aside of as much money as possible that passes through our bank accounts. So insidious are these myths that many readers will likely be shocked and reflexively reject the contrarian myth-busting concepts outlined in this book. But I urge you to read on with an open mind.

To be blunt, financial freedom—*sustainable* financial freedom, that is—isn't gained by having hoarded or simply acquired a huge stash of money. Just look to the lottery winners, professional athletes, high-profile actors and rock stars that have gone bankrupt despite having had tens of millions of dollars in their possession at some point in their lives.

Financial freedom is having established sustainable positive cash flow (ideally from multiple sources) that requires little to no additional input of our time going forward. By establishing this recurring positive cash flow, our time is then freed up to do whatever it is that we want... or nothing at all.

Why now is the right time for this book

I felt like this book was already out there, formless, floating in the ether, and chose me to write it, rather than me being the one choosing to write *it*—like I was simply the conduit through which this book chose to manifest itself in the world. Just kidding.

I felt compelled to write this book at this particular time, because there is a disturbing amount of contradictory beliefs about money these days, both on a macro and individual scale. While money isn't everything, it ranks right up there with oxygen, as the late great leadership and self-development guru, Zig Ziglar, once said.

Many people subscribe to the notion that "the rich are getting richer and the poor are getting poorer." On the one hand, news articles about, and evidence of, people running out of money in retirement are not only commonplace, but seem to be increasing in frequency. Take for example, the article published by Forbes in March of 2012 that talks about the growing reality of aging parents running out of money. According to a study conducted by Vanderbilt University between April 1993 to November 2002, lottery winners are twice more likely to claim bankruptcy than non-lottery winners.

On the other hand, according to an article published by The Economist in January 2011, there were more millionaires in the world than the entire population of Australia at the time. No doubt the disparity between those two numbers has grown since then. Between November 2008 and October 2014, the U.S. Federal Reserve added over $4.5 trillion U.S. dollars to the money supply. And, at the time of this writing, the S&P 500 stock index has been soaring at record high levels since March 2013 never before seen in all of human history—a fact that has seen very little attention in the media.

So, is the problem truly a lack of money or is the problem a lack of knowledge of how to generate and keep our fair share of money? I believe the problem sits squarely in our misguided beliefs in the seven money myths contained within this book.

Pattern recognition

As a financial consultant from 2004 to 2012, I estimate I must have conducted over a thousand personal financial reviews, both formal and informal. As you can imagine, over those eight years I spent tens of thousands of hours thinking about, talking about and working on people's personal finances. After noticing more than a few patterns during these household financial interviews I started asking questions.

I started questioning what the purpose of it all was—work, money, taxes and personal finances in general. I began to take special notice of what people used money for, why they wanted it, why they worked for it, how they earned it, how they saved it, how they spent it, how they invested it, how they protected it, how they donated it, how they shared it, how they hoarded it and often times how they were controlled by it.

I took special notice of how and why some people seemed to always have lots of money while others always seemed to have a shortage of it. I observed them and asked them question after question. I was fascinated by the differences between what certain people were able to manifest and what certain other people were not able to manifest when it came to money. I learned how they thought about money, how they respected it or didn't respect it. I learned about how they learned about money and who they learned it from.

Everything I learned about money...

There is a wonderful poem printed on a poster that I once bought when I was in university. It was called, "All I Really Need to Know I Learned in Kindergarten" by Robert Fulghum. It's a wonderfully poignant and almost nostalgic poem that points out that the basic lessons we learned at the beginning of our schooling still apply to us as adults—everything, that is, except lessons about money.

When I started as a financial planner, I knew almost nothing about money, except for the instructions I followed in the government booklets we used to get at the post office for completing our income tax returns. Everything I learned about money I learned from other people—either from observing them as their financial planner or from being formally trained by trainers, mentors and coaches. Bill Gates famously began his TED talk in May 2013 by saying, "Everyone needs a coach. It doesn't matter whether you're a basketball player, a tennis player, a gymnast, or a bridge player."

Most people never think to get formally trained in money matters, yet it's painfully obvious that those that do get formally trained do relatively better than those that do not.

I left the traditional financial planning industry in June 2012 after receiving and successfully implementing some of this higher level training that I refer to. From then until now and going forward, I continue to pursue higher levels in personal finance and real world investment training, because I happened upon yet another painfully simple pattern: The more real world investment training I received, the better I did financially. Pretty crazy, right?

Dual roles: Consumers versus Producers

In order for us to move to the next level of this economic money game, we need to use a different set of strategies. In school, although the concepts we learned in grade one will help us to an extent, we need a whole other set of higher level concepts in order to graduate high school. But before we get into some of those strategies, we need to understand a critical bit of context.

We need to understand the basic duality of the roles each and every one of us plays in the world of money. These two basic roles are that of consumer and producer. Other ways to look at these two roles is employee versus employer, and in sports, player versus owner. We cannot have one without the other. Keep in mind, however, that society is not split 50/50 between these two roles. The split is more like a 99/1 percent split, respectively.

In colloquial terms, most of the time what's good for consumers is bad for producers and vice versa. Think about this: Increased competition is good for consumers, because it forces producers to lower their prices. Obviously, lower prices are bad for producers and may even put them out of business.

Monopolies or oligopolies, where there are only one or very few producers but many consumers, tend to result in higher prices. Obviously, higher prices are less appealing to consumers yet favourable for producers.

A true producer is someone that *owns* a means of production. A producer usually has other people running the actual system of production. A producer either manages the system or has others manage the system while the producer continues to retain ownership. A consumer, on the other hand, is someone whose only means of production is their physical time or attention colloquially called "work." A sure indicator of a consumer is one that must trade her time for money in the form of salary or wages.

Most of us are both consumers and producers in some way. The fact is that those of us that are more producer than consumer tend to enjoy greater financial stability and sustainability with less physical effort—a situation that I presume is appealing to you if you are reading this book.

Basic, traditional, common financial advice is meant for an audience of consumers. This book is intended for those that wish to begin the transition from being mostly a consumer to being mostly a producer for the benefits that come with it. I expand upon this concept in chapter one, "Myth #1: The Time is Money Myth." Keep this consumer versus producer context in mind as you continue to digest the counter-intuitive concepts contained within the rest of this book.

The answer you seek in a single word

Speaking of time, I know that yours is precious. So, here's where I draw a line in the sand and you decide whether or not you and I are going to continue this conversation.

In a word, the answer you seek is *entrepreneurialism*. It's the one-size-fits-all answer to all of your financial woes. Whether you accept or reject the concepts in this book will solely depend on whether or not you are, or are willing to start, thinking like an entrepreneur.

I'm not saying go out and quit your job tomorrow. No, of course not. But I *am* telling you right now that none of these concepts will make any sense to you if you are not willing to "start something new", which is coincidentally the direct English translation of the French word *entrepreneur*. "Entrepren-*new*-er" = "Start something-*new*-eh?" (I really don't know if that's true, probably it's not, but it sounds good).

If you're not at least open to doing something different with your financial life other than earning a salary or trading hours for dollars, then please, put this book down and slowly step away. The contrarian money concepts in this book will probably just serve to upset you and life is too short to be upset, wouldn't you agree?

But, if you're already upset, say, with your job or with living paycheque to paycheque (or paycheck to paycheck if you's Amurican) or how far away you are from ever being able to retire, then this just might be a great read for you. And you just may feel compelled to hug and kiss this book and recommend it to all your friends even before you're done reading it. This would totally not be weird at all and would be perfectly acceptable—even encouraged—forms of behaviour.

So, if you're still with me, I invite you to read on.

What you are about to learn

After designing so many traditional financial plans in my previous career, that included very specific personal and household budgets, I came to understand why budgeting in the traditional sense simply doesn't work for most people. I discovered the one critical element that meant the difference between a successful budget and an exercise in futility. I talk about this one critical element in chapter three, "Myth #3: The Budgeting Myth" and how we can make budgeting truly work for us.

Before I became more enlightened, I had advised all of my clients that they must always try harder and harder to spend less and save more. I used to say "You can never save too much," and, "The more you save, the earlier you can retire." I didn't realize that you can actually take the act of saving too far and you can definitely save too much to the point that it can make you overly obsessive to the point of neurosis. I've seen this first-hand more times than I care to recall. I also didn't realize at the time that the retirement we see in TV commercials is very different from the retirement that most people are realistically heading towards. I have since learned better. I share these realizations and personal revelations with you in chapter two, "Myth #2: The Saving (and *Savings*) Myth," and chapter five, "Myth #5: The Retirement Myth."

I had also advised my clients to pay down all their debts and to stay away from debt in any way shape or form as much as humanly possible. Years later, I learned that, ironically, debt can actually make you wealthier. And, in the hands of an educated investor, debt is actually a safer and more efficient alternative to cash. Crazy stuff, right? I expand upon this higher level concept in chapter four, "Myth #4: The Debt Myth."

This book is meant to be read in a linear fashion. I purposely made each chapter as brief and concise as possible, so that the entire book could actually be read in one sitting if you feel inspired to do so. Once you've read the earlier chapters, you will be better equipped to understand the surprising realities of both The Net Worth Myth and The Home Equity Myth in chapters six and seven, respectively.

When all is said and done...

After you finish reading this book, I hope that you will consider yourself the fortunate beneficiary of my many years and countless hours of observation, analysis and contemplations surrounding personal finances. It is my goal that this book will help you shave at least eight years off of your own long term financial goals, precisely the amount of time I spent as a "traditional" financial planner, and alter the course of your own family tree starting with you and continuing your legacy with your children and grandchildren.

I recommend that you read this book at least twice. The more the better. Repetition is key. When all is said and done, let's make sure more is "done" than "said." Let's make sure we actually DO something with the knowledge contained within this book.

Bonus material

I have included a few juicy bonuses and free learning modules in a secret are of my website exclusively for readers of this book at CoachRoel.com/URBonuses worth thousands of dollars. If put into practice, these bonuses could truly be worth hundreds of thousands for both you and your progeny for years to come. ("Gee, delusions of grandeur much, Roel?")

Let's get started, already!

Congratulations on challenging the status quo by questioning traditional personal finance basics and opening your mind to the true nature of these insidious myths. I truly believe that just like your favourite sweater, once a mind is expanded it never goes back to being the same ever again.

Myth #1:
The Time Is Money Myth
I Owe. I Owe. It's Off to Work I Go.

> *"There is nothing more demoralizing than a small but, adequate income."*
> Edmund Wilson

In the movie *The Matrix*, my favourite character was Laurence Fishburne's Morpheus. He was the guy that offered Keanu Reeves' character, Neo, a choice between the blue pill and the red pill. The blue pill would allow Neo to go back to living the illusion that is the Matrix. The red pill would free his mind to see the world as it truly was.

My Morpheus was my first real estate mentor. He asked me to fill in the blank, "Time is, _____" To which I enthusiastically responded with a huge grin "MONEY!" Exasperated, he declared that we had a lot of work to do. He proceeded to teach me how my belief that time is money is precisely the reason why I wasn't living the life I wanted to live. To say that I was confused by this statement would be like saying Mount Everest is a bit of an obstruction.

Oh, I was making money alright. I was making over six figures and I was an award-winning division director and financial consultant at the time. I didn't know how to tell him that I was kind of a big deal. Or, so I convinced myself to believe. On the outside, in my workplace, I was seen as successful. I had responsibility. I had status amongst my peers and I was on the short list for a promotion. I had earned exotic incentive trips to Tokyo and Rome and… downtown Toronto. All the while, I was finding myself with less and less free time. The pressures and expectations to grow and develop both my client base, my assets under management and my consultant division meant less and less free time for me.

My mentor helped me realize that time is much more than money.

What is "The Time is Money Myth"?

The Time is Money Myth is the belief that the only decent way to earn money is to earn it in exchange for a hard day's work. A decent wage for an honest day's work, they say. It is the belief that the best way to make money is to trade our time for it in the form of a job earning a salary or an hourly wage. We wear our occupation on our sleeve like a badge of honour. It is also the misguided belief that we can sell our time for money in order to achieve financial freedom.

Believing that time is money is the number one greatest roadblock between you and financial freedom. It is the greatest obstacle blocking you on your way to wealth.

If you feel that your personal financial freedom is still several years away, or that financial freedom is difficult to achieve, or worse, impossible to achieve, then it's because you too are a victim of The Time is Money Myth. You can never have financial freedom as long as the only way you know how to generate money is by trading your precious time for it. If this sounds like you or the beliefs you hold and you're feeling frustrated because of them, then consider this chapter; Lo… consider this entire book essential reading as you free yourself from these psychological chains and shackles and be oppressed no more! But, seriously…

Where did the phrase "time is money" come from?

Many of us don't know that the phrase, "time is money," is most commonly attributed to Benjamin Franklin in his letter "Advice to a Young Tradesman, Written by an Old One" (21 July 1748). Although, if you want to be anal about it, the phrase was first cited in "Free Thinker, Volume 3" Citation: 1719 May 18, The Free-Thinker, Page 128 (GN Page 119), Number 121, London.

Franklin said that if a man can earn 10 shillings per day, but spends half the day doing nothing, effectively, he throws away five shillings. This was just the starting point of Franklin's overall financial advice. His essay, "The Way to Wealth," suggests the first step is to make productive use of your time.

Throughout most of history, we've misinterpreted this "time is money" bit of advice to mean that the best use of one's time is to use it in exchange for money. I know that this is a misinterpretation, because of what Franklin wrote in the following paragraphs. In fact, Franklin devoted nearly three quarters of this letter to explaining credit and its use.

In the very next paragraph, Franklin said that "CREDIT is Money" too. That's a direct quote. I bet you didn't know he said that. In his Olde English way, he went on to say that credit can be used to make lots of money, but only if you know how.

I've included Benjamin Franklin's complete original letter "Advice to a Young Tradesman, Written by an Old One" at CoachRoel.com/URBonuses for your reference.

After Benjamin Franklin advised the young tradesman that credit is also money, he went on to say that money has a prolific nature, ergo credit has a prolific nature. Because Franklin made specific mention of this, I believe he didn't intend for the young tradesman to continue to trade his time for money *forever*—this is merely a way to get started. I believe Franklin's advice that time is money was more of a warning against indolence than it was the entire equation for achieving wealth.

In grade school, once you've passed grade one you wouldn't spend the rest of your life repeating grade one until you got straight As. That would be a bit silly, wouldn't it? And you certainly wouldn't continue repeating grade one aiming to get straight As every year if you got straight As the first time around. You would move on to grade two, then grade three, four and so on building upon what you learned back in grade one.

So it is with trading time for money. It's where you start. It's not where you stay. Let me repeat that: Trading time for money is only a starting point. It's something you want to progress from as soon as possible. Once you know how to trade time for money, you move on to learn more and better (read: more efficient) ways to generate money. You can always go back to trading time for money if you have to start all over again.

The subtext here is that if you know how to use money to make more money, then all the money you'll ever need will be available to you. So, what would be the use of trading your time for money after that point? None. Who would want to repeat grade one after they've already graduated high school?

Key concept: Highest and best use of money

Why do we even need money in the first place? According to Maslow's Hierarchy of Needs, the basic necessities of life are food, water, air, sleep, sex and excretion. We need money to purchase food. And some people need money to purchase sex, but that's a whole other topic altogether. Once those basic physiological needs are taken care of, Maslow postulates that we then need safety, love/belonging, esteem, self-actualization and ultimately self-transformation. He places the need for income and property within the basic safety category.

As we progress through our hierarchy of needs, we not only need money to afford ourselves these needs, but we also need the free *time* to be able to self-actualize and transform ourselves. We can have all the money in the world for our basic needs, but we need the time to be able to develop our personal relationships, to strengthen our self-esteem, to self-actualize and then to transform ourselves.

The highest and best use of money is to give us freedom and control over our time, how we spend and who we spend it with—to deepen our relationships and develop ourselves. Money is a tool, an enabler, a thing that allows us to do something of our choosing. Money is not, and should not, be the goal in and of itself.

The true measure of wealth

A person in prison is not wealthy at all, because they have absolutely no control over how they spend their time and who they spend it with except within the confines of the prison. Some would argue that a job is not that much different from being confined to a prison, albeit if only for eight hours a day, five days a week.

A person that only needs to spend a few hours per week, or per month, managing their portfolio of income-producing assets (like rental properties, online and traditional businesses, and financial assets) has much more control over how they spend their time and who they spend it with. This person is truly wealthy, but not because of the size of their bank account or how much they are "worth."

We need a real-life, pragmatic measure for wealth—context within which we can better understand and address the abundant money myths that plague us: Wealth is not measured in money; wealth is measured in *time*.

If you must work sixty, seventy, eighty hours per week to sustain your lifestyle, then you are less wealthy than the person who only needs to work six, seven or eight hours per week to achieve the same end. Period.

Remember, the highest and best use of money is to give us the freedom to choose how we spend our time and who we spend it with. The true measure of wealth, therefore, is the amount of control we have over how we choose to spend our time and the amount of control we have over who we choose to spend our time with.

Think about this: How many months forward could you continue your current lifestyle if you could no longer trade your time for money? Think about the order in which you would deplete your cash, stocks, bonds and mutual funds, if any. How long would it take to max out all of your credit cards and lines of credit? When would you start selling off your stuff online or hold a garage sale or *sales*? When would you decide to get a loan against your car, your house and then eventually be forced to sell both simply because you didn't know how to generate income aside from working at a job?

If you measure your wealth in the amount of dollars you've saved or the dollar-equivalent value of all the stuff you own, then you're SO on the wrong path.

Pop quiz:

What did the multi-millionaire say on her luxurious deathbed as she quietly prayed? "Oh, Lord. Please give me just a little more _____."

    a. Money
    b. Time

Time is not money. But, money *can be* time.

We need to flip that saying around. Instead of saying, "time is money," we should say, "money is time." Jim Carrey famously said, "I think everybody should get rich and famous and do everything they ever dreamed of so they can see that it's not the answer." How truly unsatisfying is it to buy more, bigger and nicer stuff? We should pursue money for the sole purpose of getting back our time! If you think of your job, your investments and your education within the context of attaining more and better control over your *time*, how you spend it and who you spend it with, I guarantee your daily actions will become much, much clearer.

Rather than trade our time for money, we should be trading our money for time. It's true that all the money in the world can't buy us the ability to go back in time (at least not yet), but money efficiently generated, wisely invested and effectively managed *can* ensure that we have ample control over our time going forward.

Think about this the next time you're tempted to stay late at work whether it's self-inflicted or whether your boss or the company culture expects it of you. Think about this the next time you miss a memorable milestone with your child like their first step, first recital or first base hit. Think about this the next time you feel deathly ill and you feel guilty about calling in sick. The world won't stop spinning if you miss a day of work or quit your job altogether. No one is *that* important. But for those that matter most in your life, *their* world is definitely adversely affected whenever you're not there.

What's the answer?

If time is not money, and we accept that money's highest and best use is to afford us freedom and control over our time, then what is time? Well, my friend, as my Morpheus—my first real estate mentor—likes to put it, "Time is EVERYTHING." Time is the most important thing, the most precious thing. It must be cherished and protected and spent as wisely as possible.

Our time on this earth is finite, unless you believe in reincarnation. But even then, good luck trying to continue as a baby, where you left off as an octogenarian. For all practical reasons, we have one life to live. I know this time and money discussion sounds very airy fairy and new age philosophical, but it's a key distinction that we must grasp in order to understand what is truly keeping us from living the life we deserve.

But how do we know if we are spending our time wisely or not? We can't always be sitting around a pool or on a tropical beach sipping Mai Tai's and waxing philosophical with friends, can we?

Hmm, why not? That sounds pretty awesome, actually. Seriously. Maybe not every single day and maybe not right now, but if that would truly make you happy, why not make tropical-beach-sitting and Mai-Tai-sipping with family and friends your ultimate goal?

What's the first thing you think about when trying to plan for your next vacation? "When can I take the time off [from work]?" right? And "How much time can I take off [from work]?" Right?

When contemplating a new job one of the first things you think about is "How much vacation time will I get?" Although, any keen applicant worth hiring would never ask this question during their first interview.

Do you remember what it feels like to be laying on the beach knowing that your employer is still paying you vacation time? As you lie there on your beach chair under the shade of a huge umbrella, sand between your toes, listening to the sound of the ocean waves lapping on the shore, you feel calm and relaxed knowing you received a direct deposit of a few thousand dollars into your bank account from your employer just before you left for vacation. And, you know you feel safe and secure knowing you're going to receive another direct deposit right after you return from vacation.

That's what it feels like to have money working for you. It's definitely not the same thing, but being on a paid vacation is like having temporary passive income. You're no longer trading your time for the money to come in. You've put in the work previously and now the money is coming in on its own, if only for one or two weeks per year. But what if you could put in the work today and get paid for the rest of your life? Aha! NOW, we're on to something.

A time-is-not-money thought-experiment

But I'm getting off topic. A great way to quickly determine if you are spending your time wisely or not is to do the one-thousand times test in your head. If you are doing something and in your head you multiply that action or activity by one-thousand, you'll quickly know whether it's a wise use of your time. Let's say you are driving to work in the morning through rush hour traffic. Multiply that by one-thousand. Do you like the result? I'm guessing "no." Now, let's say you are teaching your child how to kick a soccer ball or walking hand-in-hand with your life partner as you explore the streets of a foreign city.

Multiply that by one-thousand. Do you like the result? Shame on you if your answer is anything but a resounding "YES!"

Of course you wouldn't actually spend a thousand hours doing any of these things, but it helps to put into perspective whether something is truly worth your time.

"Yeah, but it's not always that simple."

But those are obvious scenarios, you might say. So, what about grey areas like if you are working late one evening in order to finish a presentation that could earn you a handsome commission or bonus the next morning should the client or your boss buy into your proposal? Multiply that whole scenario by one-thousand. Do you like the result? Well, it depends. Did you burn out from all those late nights? Did you miss out on family time? Did the huge monetary rewards outweigh the personal sacrifices? I think if you actually considered the one-thousand times factor, the answer would be that you did not like the result.

"Surely, sacrificing a little family time is okay, right?"

You might say that working late once in a while for the potential of a big monetary payout would be worth it. Although, that's a slippery slope, I would agree with you if it's for your own business and you're going to benefit from it in recurring revenue, then yes. But if it's for your employer and it's only for a one-time big payout, or worse if it's a regular part of your job, then I would say no, it's definitely not worth it.

Why? Because, although the latter is trading time for a big payout, it's trading time for a one-time big payout. The former is trading time for multiple payouts AND you own it. See the difference?

And, how many times are you actually sacrificing time with loved ones to work on just one more project or just one more proposal? Is the time sacrifice truly temporary or has it gone on for far too long already?

If you adhere to the ideal that time is money during your working years, your most productive years, then where does that leave you during your retirement years? What if you fall short with your retirement savings, but you are no longer physically able to sell your time for money? Where's the line where sacrificing a little family time becomes sacrificing too much family time for the sake of work and money?

By doing nothing other than trade our time for money during our physically capable years and refusing to learn any other way of making money, we place ourselves in an extremely precarious position when we are no longer physically employable.

Final words on The Time is Money Myth

Since most of us live in that in-between area, what do we do? We can start by understanding that time is NOT money. Money can buy you time and time is the most important thing. We can start by thinking of ways to spend our time on things that will generate us money continually with little to no additional input of our time.

We must not waste our most physically capable years deferring the life we want to live until sometime decades into the future. What if we didn't have ten, twenty, thirty more years to plan? What if we only gave ourselves a hard stop deadline of five years to build the life we truly want to live? How would we choose to conduct ourselves, approach our work and invest our time and money then? Would we spend more time working a job or spend our free time learning how to do something different? Necessity is the mother of creativity.

We must learn how to not work for money even though we are currently perfectly capable of doing so. We must prepare ourselves for the years when we can no longer work for money by putting mechanisms in place today that will generate income for us with little to no additional input of our time or our physical presence.

We can start by just simply questioning our assumptions about time and money, why we complain about not having enough of the former and why we sacrifice so much for the latter.

That's as good a place to start as any.

Myth #2:
The Saving (and *Savings*) Myth
Why Cash is Not King

> "*What happened when the cat swallowed a coin?*
> *There was money in the kitty.*"
> Anonymous

Sméagol spent his early years living with his extended family and his grandmother. Déagol was his cousin, and on Sméagol's birthday, they went fishing in the Gladden Fields north of the mountains. After being pulled into the water by a large fish, Déagol found a gold ring. Almost immediately, Sméagol fell to the power of the ring and demanded it as a birthday present. When Déagol refused, Sméagol went into a savage rage and fought with Déagol over the ring, strangled him to death and took the ring as his own.

Sméagol was quickly corrupted further by the ring and banished by his people. Kicked out by his grandmother, he was forced to find a home in a cave in the Misty Mountains. The ring's malignant influence twisted and contorted his body, as well as his mind. He called it his "Precious" or his "Birthday Present," the latter as a justification for killing Déagol. This hideous version of Sméagol became known as Gollum derived from his disgusting gurgling and choking cough.

The Hobbit and The Lord of the Rings fans will instantly recognize this character. This image of Sméagol-turned-Gollum is a caricature of what we become when simple fancy becomes obsession. It is what comes to my mind when we take the act of saving too far, when we become "cheap" and obsessed with saving money and over-protective of our savings.

I will expose the Savings (*and Savings*) Myth and save you (pun intended) from falling victim to this myth. I will clarify what saving (and *savings*) is good for and what it's not good for. I will enlighten you as to why saving is good for some financial goals, but terrible for most others. And, finally, I will outline what you can do to better achieve those financial goals.

What is "The Saving (and *Savings*) Myth"?

The Saving (and *Savings*) Myth is the belief that we can save our way to wealth, financial freedom or any other major financial goal. It is the belief that the act of saving money is the one-size-fits-all answer to all of our financial planning needs.

The *savings* part of the myth is the belief that the best place for our emergency funds and long-term money is within a savings account—in cash or cash equivalents. Lastly, the Saving (and *Savings*) Myth is the assumption that we must first learn how to save before we can learn how to invest.

What is the true nature of money?

To put the Saving (and *Savings*) Myth into context, it would be helpful for us to first understand a bit more about the true nature of money. We must realize that money is no longer money per se. Money is debt.

No matter what country you live in, your government goes into debt by selling their treasury bills and government bonds to other governments, so that your government can print more money. These are called government-issued debt instruments. A treasury bill is basically a bunch of words that a government scribbles on a piece of paper stating that it is worth X number of that country's money. Whenever these pieces of paper are created, and sold, the issuing government prints more money. Sound like a nice little scam? I agree, especially when you realize that a government can be both the seller AND the buyer of their own debt instruments, meaning it can sell debt to itself. This allows them to print money ad nauseam whenever, and for however much, they feel like. Pretty nice gig.

To give it an air of official-ness, governments and central banks have dubbed this discretionary printing of money and selling to itself of government debt instruments "Quantitative Easing," google it. It's been happening for years. In short, Quantitative Easing is basically when a nation's leaders create additional money in order to stimulate their country's economy.

Here's another little fun fact that'll fry your noodle: They don't actually use physical, tangible paper anymore. I just mentioned paper to make it easier to grasp the concept. They create this so-called money on a computer and it is nothing more than a bunch of electrical charges saved on a highly secure, firewall-protected hard drive brought into existence with a few strokes by a government employee and then digitally fed into the economy. Indeed, most of the so-called money in the world today is not tangible, but only exists in this virtual manner. But, I digress.

Japan first invented the concept of "Quantitative Easing" in the early 2000s, when it was called "Credit Easing." As of this writing, the Bank of Japan said that it would print 80 trillion Japanese yen ($810 billion CAD) in 2015. Previously, it was *only* printing ¥60 to ¥70 trillion per year (that was a bit of sarcasm, in case you missed it).

Around this same time, the U.S. has just completed printing over $4.5 trillion USD between November 2008 and October 2014, alone. On January 22, 2015, the European Central Bank announced that it would print €60 billion ($81.8 billion CAD) per month. Starting March 2015, the printing of Euros was planned to last until September 2016 at the earliest with a total QE of at least €1.1 trillion ($1.5 trillion CAD).

The money in your wallet and in your bank account is actually a promissory note created by your government on your behalf. Thus, money is debt... created out of thin air.

BUT, governments didn't actually print the majority of money in circulation today or what is called "the money supply." No, money isn't even really paper money and precious metal coins anymore. Money, today, largely exists only in digital form as electrical or magnetic charges—blips on computers. Whoa. Ponder that one for a while. It is estimated that physical paper money and coins only represent about 5% of the total world money supply. The other 95% exists only on bank hard drives. Think about how much physical cash you have in your possession at this very moment as compared to the digits representing the "money" in your bank accounts and your stocks, bonds and mutual fund accounts. Your personal ratio is probably more like 1% to 99% between tangible and intangible money, respectively. And the disparity between tangible and intangible money worldwide is only increasing as countries continue playing these currency games.

Banks, not governments, have created most of the money supply these days and continue to do so at an alarming rate. What do I mean? In a word: "fractionalized lending." I know that's two words. Just trying to make a dry topic even a little entertaining. If a bank has one dollar on deposit, it can lend out ten times that amount in credit. Just prior to the sub-prime mortgage bubble bursting in 2007, that factor was up to forty and fifty times for some U.S. banks.

Money is not money anymore, because it is no longer backed by any hard asset, like gold. That ended when President Nixon took the U.S. dollar off the gold standard in 1971. Since then, money became a fiat currency—meaning, it is no longer backed by anything except the confidence that someone will accept it for payment for the amount that you both agree that it is worth.

Key concept: Money is energy

Whether we like it or not, money is always moving no matter how much we try to stop it. Even when we try to save it in cash and we think it is not going anywhere, the potential energy of money is actually dissipating through the degrading effects of inflation much the same way a battery gradually loses its stored electrical charge over time. We simply cannot stop the movement of money.

Rather than try to *stop* the movement of money, we must constantly strive to improve our skill at *managing* the movement of money. Money is energy and energy is infinite. To try to contain energy for long periods of time is an inefficient use of said energy. If we ignore the infinite nature of money by trying to hinder its movement we condemn ourselves to be ever fearful of running out of money altogether.

When we buy our first home, for example, we save a little bit of money as our down payment and then we borrow the rest. That little bit of down payment money is used to "attract" a lot more money in the form of a mortgage, so that we can buy that first home much sooner rather than later. A little bit of money, combined with our good credit history, can be used to give us the use of a lot more money. This is money in motion and is a very efficient use of money.

It would be ridiculous to wait until we have saved all the cash necessary in order to buy the house outright. That would be a highly *inefficient* use of money. Most of us would probably never reach the goal of homeownership if we tried to do it this way.

Saving takes money out of circulation thus stops it from moving. Money, put in motion, attracts more money. Saving little by little for major financial goals is tremendously inefficient and hardly effective. The act of saving and maintaining savings, hoarding, is the lowest and worst use of money. It is not cash that is king, but cash *flow*.

Don't misinterpret this money-needs-to-move thing as an excuse for you to go out and rack up your consumer debt and spend all of your cash indiscriminately. It's true that if you put money in motion this way that it will attract more money. It's just that money that is put into motion via consumer spending attracts money to the vendors, the banks and the credit card companies, and not to you. Exorbitant consumer spending and the racking up of consumer debt balances that never seem to get paid down are grossly inefficient uses of money. This is how people get money to move *away* from them.

While the highest and best use of money is to give us control over our time, how we spend it and who we spend it with, the most efficient and productive use of money is to use it to attract more money. If we can learn how to get money to make more and more money, then we will have no need to trade our time for it anymore and we will have little fear that will scare us into hoarding (saving) money, thus eventually affording us total control over our time.

What do people save for?

By now, it should be starting to become clear how futile it is to try to save or hoard money over the long term when its value is slowly, but surely (and systematically), being deteriorated by our government. But in case the top-down perspective is not quite sinking in yet, let's take a look from the bottom-up perspective.

Generally, we have been taught to save for anything we may want to buy or spend on in the future. We save for things like a new TV, a vacation, buying a house or car, a rainy day fund and retirement to name just a few. Unfortunately, saving (and *savings*) is considered the blanket solution to every single financial goal no matter the scope or the time frame. After all, "a penny saved is a penny earned," n'est pas? Wrong. A saying like this keeps people from ever achieving financial freedom. Those that master saving money are typically less financial free (and more tied to their jobs) than those that master the movement of money (like those that create jobs).

Clarification of what saving is good for

Saving is only good for planning low- to medium-priced, short-term financial expenditures. Period. A New TV, annual vacations, an engagement ring or splurge fund (for pampering yourself) are good examples of things where saving is an appropriate strategy.

Saving is good for not overspending. Saving is good for not going into consumer debt. Saving is good for not going bankrupt and for keeping yourself above the poverty line. You can't be poor if you've been building up your savings and have no consumer debt.

But, are you playing the game to not lose (to not be poor) or are you playing to win (to be wealthy)?

Clarification of what saving is *not* good for

Saving is not good for long-term financial goals or large major purchases. Saving is not a good way to prepare to start your own business. Saving is not a good way to buy real estate. Saving is a terrible way to prepare for retirement and a terrible way to grow our money. *Saving* is not *investing*.

You can't save your way to wealth. Unfortunately, this is exactly what society has us believe we can and should do. The reality is that those that I have observed that have actually been successful at saving up a significant amount of money have lived a very frugal, almost miserly, and uneventful life only to continue to live a very frugal, almost miserly, and uneventful life in retirement for fear of losing the money they'd successfully hoarded.

What is wrong with saving money?

There's nothing inherently wrong, per se, with saving money if the interpretation you're referring to is "not frivolously spending." "Not frivolously spending" is of course a good thing. No doubt about that. But that's not what I'm talking about here. I'm talking about when savers take saving too far, like on a Gollum level. And it doesn't take much before *saving* money turns into *hoarding* money.

On a macro level, it's easier to understand why money must move. If governments and businesses all hoarded cash and stopped moving money the global financial system would grind to a halt. Actually, it would collapse in spectacular fashion. When money doesn't move around the economy we see massive drops in the financial and real estate markets, unemployment rates go up and general social unrest increases. Sounds a lot like the first decade of this millennium where we saw two major drops in the stock market and youth protests taking to the streets in Europe due to lack of jobs.

On an individual level, money needs to move as well. Having a balance of cash should be the favourable by-product of running a surplus. Having a balance of cash should not be the result of the intentional systematic removal of cash from cash flow, i.e. saving.

What is inflation and how does it affect savings?

Governments print money in order to stimulate the economy. From the opposite angle, this means that there isn't enough money moving around, so they print more of it. The adverse effect of all this money printing is that for those of us that hold onto our cash money for too long are losing purchasing power. I'll outline the positive effects of all this money printing in the chapter on The Debt Myth. This gradual loss of purchasing power is called inflation and it is not an accident.

Inflation is a goal—a bona fide government mandated financial goal. Governments actually aim to achieve a "healthy" inflation rate of 2% to 3% per year. Again, let's take a look at this from the opposite angle. This means that the purchasing power of your dollars, pounds and pesos is decreasing by a "healthy" 2% to 3% per year. Compound inflation rates are like compound interest rates, but flipped upside down. Compound inflation rates cut exponentially deeper and deeper each year into the purchasing power of your money.

A weaker currency is appealing to many governments for several reasons. A weaker currency artificially increases demand for exports. By the same token, a weaker currency deters imports. This is good for the domestic economy, because it leads to more production and employment. A weaker currency will boost tourist business and again, by the same token, deter locals from traveling abroad. A weaker currency also makes a country more appealing to foreign investors bringing even more money into the country.

Probably the most appealing thing for governments to weaken their currencies is that it makes it easier for them to pay off their national debts. Over time, printing more money essentially cancels much of a government's debts.

While it wouldn't be fair to say that governments purposely aim to decrease their citizens' purchasing power, they definitely know that their pursuit of inflation has the invariable side effect of reducing the purchasing power of those who have hoarded cash.

There is a mini-myth surrounding inflation as well. If you simply google the definition of "core inflation"—this is the inflation that you see quoted on the news—you'll be shocked to discover that not everything is included in the calculation of core inflation. Core inflation and the CPI (Consumer Price Index) both refer to the same thing. Neither one includes food and energy in its calculation. The increase in prices for these two categories alone is easily remembered in recent history. True inflation, including food and energy, is estimated at more than 8% per year in recent years.

When we witness the prices of things going up, are they really going up or is the purchasing power of our money going down? Maybe the true value of things is actually staying the same, but because the value of our money is actually deteriorating it creates the illusion that prices are going up. Not maybe. It is.

Is money scarce or not?

Money is supposed to be relatively scarce. That's the reason why money has value, because compared to air, dust and belly button lint, it is relatively scarce. But, if governments keep creating debt out of thin air and printing money indefinitely, and if banks are multiplying every new dollar ten-fold, money is increasingly less scarce. Thus, saving and accumulating your money in a savings account is only good for short term goals where the effects of inflation can barely be noticed.

Over the long term, it would be best to NOT keep our money sitting in cash, unless we are okay with our long term cash savings dying a slow and predictable death. In this sense, long-term cash is definitely NOT king, but more like a sitting duck in the cross-hairs of inflation.

Most recent estimates put the world's physical and non-physical money supply at over $70 trillion USD. Money is anything but scarce.

What's so bad about maintaining an emergency fund?

Some of the better savers justify keeping a separate savings account by designating it as an emergency fund. I used to recommend this strategy to my clients as well, when I was a new financial planner. But then I realized that several years could go by and an emergency might never come up.

Every day that passes equates to another day of opportunity lost where we could have used our savings for some other form of investing. Every day that passes the purchasing power of our savings decreases. The idle cash would lose significant purchasing power. Plus, it would take several years for someone to build up enough of an emergency fund to be worthwhile.

A better alternative would be to apply for an unsecured line of credit and instantly have access to a few thousand dollars in case of an emergency—to be used ONLY for an emergency. It wouldn't cost anything if we ended up not using it. All we would need to do is place a transaction on it once every twelve months or so to keep it active. Then we could free up the cash previously set aside for emergencies to invest in something that produced cash flow.

Do we have to be a saver before we can be an investor?

The sophisticated investor and the master saver require two totally different mentalities. The saver mentality causes people to think of money as a scarce resource—something to be stockpiled, hoarded and prevented from flowing. The assumption is that money is hard to come by. The investor mentality is quite the opposite. It requires us to think of money as abundant and in constant motion. The investor mentality requires us to think of ways we can get money to move (towards us) rather than stop moving (away from us).

If we start off trying to become a master saver, then it will be very difficult to make the change in mindset to become a sophisticated investor.

What can we do instead of *saving* for the long-term?

If a contemplated purchase is a legitimate business expense, borrow the money to buy it. Finance it. Deduct the interest as a business expense. Just make sure you can still pay the interest expense. Just because you can write it off, meaning deduct both the purchase price and the interest expense, doesn't mean you can afford the monthly debt repayments.

Business expenses are tax deductible in most countries, but you'll have to consult a specialist in your country to be sure what is considered a business expense and what is not. If you're not in business, then start one. Yes, it's that simple. Learn how to become more tax-efficient by becoming even part-time self-employed or a small business owner.

If a contemplated purchase can be considered an investment with the potential to earn interest, dividend or business income, borrow the money to purchase the investment. Put another way, don't save to invest—borrow to invest. The interest cost of borrowing to invest this way is also tax deductible in Canada and in most countries. See line 221 of your Canadian income tax return. This is where you indicate your total tax deductible interest expenses.

So, what's the answer?

If money isn't money anymore, and money is essentially debt and energy and infinite, what can we do with this knowledge? Understand first that money is also currency, from the Latin origins meaning "something that moves." I just made that up. But, it has to move nonetheless. Like water, money becomes stale and even poisonous if it isn't allowed to move. Money is moving, working, attracting more money when it is properly invested. Money only begets money when the *holder*—the person, the manager—knows how to beget money. Money is not moving or working when it is stuck in a bank account, a Guaranteed Investment Certificate (GIC) if you're in Canada, a Certificate of Deposit (CD) if you're in the U.S. or other cash-equivalent while inflation steadily eats away at it. I affectionately refer to GICs and CDs as "Guaranteed *Inflation* Certificates" and "Certificates of *Depreciation.*" I know you're going to steal my jokes. It's okay. I stole them from someone else, so go ahead.

We must hold ourselves to a higher standard and think of ourselves as investors rather than savers. Master investors, or active sophisticated investors, know how to manage the movement of money. Whereas, master savers, or passive novice investors, only know how to try to stop the movement of money. It doesn't take any skill, talent or education to essentially destroy money or cause money to die a slow death in this manner.

On the other hand, it takes vision, creativity, applied knowledge and dedication to grow our investments in order to fund the lifestyle we truly deserve to live.

Undiscovered Riches™

Myth #3:
The Budgeting Myth
Why is There Too Much Month At The End Of The Money?

> *"Studies show that 5 out 4 adults have trouble with numbers."*
> Roel Sarmago

When I was at university I remember receiving the course syllabus at the beginning of each semester. The syllabus contained the due dates of each and every assignment and exam that was required to be completed successfully in order to achieve a passing grade. I would scan the entire syllabus and transfer each due date and exam date into my "Day Runner" (remember, those?). I would proceed to write down the dates when I would begin each assignment, so that I would have enough time to do a great job on each one. I would even make a mental note to start working on each assignment early, so that I could complete each assignment early, so that I could always be ahead for the entire semester. I would follow the same protocol for planning out my study times for each exam.

At least, that's what I wrote down on paper.

The reality would turn out to be quite different each and every time. The early start date in my head for working on my first assignment would come and go. Next, the scheduled start date that I had set for myself would come and go. Finally, with a day or two left (usually, a day) before my assignment was due, or my exam date, I would pull the invariable coffee-infused all-nighter and complete whatever I needed to complete or cram-study whatever I needed to study at the very last minute—most of the time.

I couldn't figure out why my elegant study plan didn't work. On paper, it looked as flawless as could be. The dates and blocks of time all fit perfectly. I even added buffer days here and there in case I needed more time. Albert Einstein would've been impressed. But for whatever reason, things would never work out according to my plan.

What is "The Budgeting Myth"?

As part of the financial planning process I would do a personal financial review. Part of this review included an exercise to determine a person's goals and concerns. The personal financial review was basically a question and answer interview where I would ask people what their monthly expenses were and how much assets and liabilities they had. One of the common goals was to create a budget, which was a nice way of saying finding a way for them to spend less, so that they could invest more in their mutual funds with me.

Traditional budgeting starts with listing down all your expenses. Sometimes off the top of your head. Sometimes going into bank statements and credit card statements. Or a combination of all of the above. Then, totalling up all those expenses and comparing it to your income. Usually, getting your income from your paystubs or your bank statements.

The problem is that this exercise would usually result in one of two ways: Once in a while, the client would list more expenses than income. This outcome was rare. While most people know they spend more than they earn, few can actually come close to understanding why. Most often, the client would list fewer expenses than income and wonder why they have no savings to show for it. I would ask them if their bank account was growing by that much and most would say "no." At that point they would realize there were a lot more expenses unaccounted for and they really had no idea where their money was going.

The Budgeting Myth doesn't apply to people that are naturally effective at managing their personal spending habits. It applies to those that over-spend or feel that there's never enough money to do the things they really want to do. The Budgeting Myth applies to those that, ironically, need to budget the most.

The Budgeting Myth is the belief that writing down a plan where all the numbers fit nicely is all you need to ensure your expenses don't exceed your income. It is the belief that focusing on what you cannot spend and limiting what you can spend will actually help you spend less. It is the belief that simply adjusting our daily purchase decisions alone will help us achieve long-term financial freedom. It is the belief that we can stick to a budget plan beyond a few weeks simply because we've written it down.

Why do we try to budget?

We prepare a budget for several reasons: To pay down debt; to have more money to spend on other things; to save up to make a major purchase like a vacation, a car or a down payment on a house; to have extra money to put away for retirement.

The act of preparing a traditional budget feels good. Although, few of us actually take the time to prepare one and fewer of us still actually stick to it. For many, it represents our entire financial plan. It feels like we're actually doing something, albeit just on paper at the time. Then we go about our life all happy and eventually forget about it and slip back into our old habits.

Why does traditional budgeting not work?

For a very small minority, traditional budgeting actually works. Meaning, they are able to stay within the spending limits that they set for themselves in each category. This is a very rare breed—people who are naturally frugal and disciplined with their money. For them, they don't even really need to write up a formal budget. They are natural non-spenders as it is.

What I've found with traditional budgeting is that the majority of us can't stick to a budget for very long—at least not long enough to realize any significant benefit.

There are many reasons why traditional budgeting doesn't work. The biggest reason is because we see budgeting as the goal in and of itself, e.g. "My goal is to spend less. My goal is to live within my means." Those are shitty goals. Is there anything exciting about spending less and living within your means? No. Spending less and living within your means are not goals, just like investing and making lots of money are not goals. They are objectives that may help you achieve your ultimate goals.

Traditional budgeting doesn't work, because it feels restrictive. Because the word budget implies unappealing hard work. Because people don't like to make sacrifices. Because it makes people feel depressed. Because people focus on what they can't have. Aha! Because the mere concept of budgeting itself forces people to focus on the wrong thing.

What has been the fallout when budgeting doesn't work?

When people are trying to budget, they're already depressed as it is. When budgeting doesn't work, they feel even more depressed. People tend to binge spend after budgeting doesn't work. A lot of people end up going deeper into debt after budgeting doesn't work.

The one critical element

Ironically, the difference between a successful budget and an exercise in futility has very little to do with the numbers. On paper, budgeting makes total sense. It's logical. It's simple math. Objectively, most would agree that a budget makes sense.

If you've tried to stick to a budget and failed, especially if you've failed multiple times, you'll kick yourself when I tell the reason. Better yet, let me kick you. Just kidding. Or am I?

Here's the big reveal: The one critical element that will determine successful budget-sticking is (dramatic pause)... MOTIVATION.

The smoker needs to quit smoking, but doesn't, until she decides she truly wants to quit smoking and follows through with healthier alternatives. An alcoholic needs to stop hurting her family as a result of her constant inebriation, but doesn't, until she decides she truly wants to limit her drinking and seek help. No amount of fiddling with the numbers or consulting with financial planners or credit counsellors is going to work until the over-spender finally decides there is no other alternative than to reign in his indiscriminate spending.

What principals do I need to follow in order to budget more effectively?

Focus on what you want rather than what you don't want. People usually want to budget their money or follow a budget because they basically feel like they're spending too much money. The word "budget" itself implies cutting down on spending. Merely wanting to spend less is not a strong enough motivator to actually spend less. Especially, if you're not already naturally frugal.

For most of us, spending too much, buying lots of stuff and living beyond our current means is something we do, because it feels good—because we don't have something else that makes us feel better. This is the reasoning behind the term "retail therapy," which many women use as an excuse to engage in indiscriminate spending when they are feeling unhappy.

We need to determine a strong enough reason *why* we should spend less. We need to get emotional, get excited about that reason. I've seen it many times in twenty-something and thirty-something year olds that previously spent 110% of their discretionary income on stuff and socializing and entertainment. Once they meet that special someone, they're spending habits turn into making dinner at home, saving for an engagement ring, saving for a wedding and saving for a down payment on a house.

We don't need to make another person our reason for reigning in our superfluous spending habits. Simply having a higher and better vision for our lives can be a good enough reason. Once we have a higher and better vision for ourselves, we no longer feel bad about having to spend less. We start to feel guilty for spending too much on lower forms of "retail" gratification.

How do I *prepare to* budget?

Determine a strong emotional goal. WHY do you want to spend less and save more? WHY do you want to live within your means? For what reason? Get excited about that goal. Then forget about spending less and saving more. Just focus on being excited about the goal you are working towards.

Start an expense diary and write down every single expense you make for just two weeks. Write down each transaction as it happens, especially the pre-authorized expenses, those are the ones easiest to forget. Don't guess. Just begin to become aware of where all your money is going as it happens.

If you've articulated for yourself an exciting enough and emotional enough "why" then you'll notice you'll start feeling a bit guilty when you make unnecessary purchases that hinder you from getting closer to your ultimate goal. If you're really excited and emotional about your "why" you may even begin to feel upset with yourself when you spend on frivolous things.

How do I actually budget more effectively?

Rather than focus on cutting things out of your budget, look for ways to trim a little bit from all your regular expenditures. E.g. If you normally order a venti cappuccino at Starbucks, order a grande or order a venti Americano or order a tall Americano or go to a less expensive coffee shop altogether. Or, you could spend a little bit more on the "nicer" coffees at the grocery store that you make at home or in the office. These would still cost less than any retail-bought coffee.

Rather than focus on the things you need to cut out, focus on alternatives that you can get excited about or at least feel good about. How can you get excited about bringing a bagged lunch to work? Start by cooking your favourite (and hopefully, healthiest) yummiest meals on Sundays—enough to last you at least the first two or three days of the week for lunches. Better if you can eventually prepare a full week's worth of lunches on Sundays, but start with at least the first two lunches of the week. That's 40% of the week's lunches shaved from your expenses, replaced by much less expensive home cooked lunches. This way, you'll look forward to bringing your lunch to work, which conveniently costs less than buying it every day. It's probably much healthier too!

Instead of saying, "I can't" or "I shouldn't," feel the empowerment of saying to yourself, "I can, but I don't need to. I have higher goals that mean more to me." Feel empowered that you do have the money to spend on those little things, but you have no use to spend on them. If your values change, you'll no longer feel you need to buy those extra little things in order to feel good about yourself. It comes back to your self-concept, your self-esteem.

Make a personal game out of budgeting. Every time you successfully complete a cost-effective alternative think of it like you're racking up points towards your high score or being one step closer to victory. And think of your high score or victory as the exciting goal you set out for yourself in the beginning.

Spend more time with like-minded people. Sometimes it's tough to spend less when your closest friends like to spend a lot. Often times overspending is attributed to social pressures. This is what the term "keeping up with the Joneses" refers to. We feel pressured to buy that nice car or go on that expensive vacation or go out to those expensive dinners. There's a joke that goes like this: "What leads most people into debt? Trying to catch up with people who are already there." It goes without saying that you will need your spouse to be on the same page.

It's easier to spend less when you hang around people that would choose to host a potluck or a backyard barbecue over going out to a fancy restaurant. Or, people that would choose to go camping over staying at a posh hotel. Those more expensive luxuries can be had when you've learned enough about money to be able to quit your day job.

Make prudent major decisions. All too often I've witnessed extremely prudent and otherwise fiscally responsible people make terrible major purchase decisions. They decide to buy the "nice" car or the "nice" house or treat themselves to a "nice" vacation. They justify it to themselves by saying they deserve it because they've worked so hard for it. In actuality, they're using the word "nice" as a way to justify a more expensive luxury that they know deep down inside isn't necessary and doesn't make fiscal sense.

You can be as frugal and as prudent as you want on a daily basis, but if you get a mortgage or finance a car that maxes out your debt servicing capacity, then no amount of monthly frugality is going to help you. Just because the financing officer approves you for a huge loan, doesn't mean you have to take it. Credit officers don't take into account how many mouths you have to feed or daycare or medication or fuel expense in your debt ratios when approving you for a loan. It's not their responsibility to take these off-balance sheet commitments into consideration. It's your responsibility.

Every once in a while, practice extreme frugality for a few a weeks. This is to remind yourself that you can actually live on very little and still be happy. Remember, this assumes you have an exciting emotionally engaging goal that you are working towards.

Make it a habit. Once your new, more cost-effective activities become habit, then the whole thing becomes effortless. You can begin to really reap the rewards. At this point, you're actually no longer budgeting. Your reasonable spending habits are simply a matter of fact for you. Then you can focus on other things like learning how to become a sophisticated investor and how to be more tax-efficient, so that you can keep more of the money that you are able to generate.

What is the conclusion?

By budgeting in this way, you're actually not budgeting in the traditional sense at all. You're habitualizing the decrease in your day to day spending. Once your decreased spending becomes a habit, it no longer requires effort and is therefore sustainable. You're no longer constantly consciously thinking about spending less or sacrificing or restricting yourself. You're not stressfully trying to avoid something bad, you're excitedly moving towards something good.

Myth #4:
The Debt Myth
Why Debt Works for Some, But Not for Most

> *"If you owe the bank $100, that's your problem.*
> *If you owe the bank $100 million, that's the bank's problem."*
> J. Paul Getty, Billionaire Oil Tycoon

Early in my financial planning career I inherited an orphaned client. His original planner had left the business long before. This client's situation presented me with a real head-scratcher that I wasn't able to figure out at the time. He had three rental properties in Sault Ste. Marie, Ontario that were all under water—meaning, the mortgage amounts owed on each of the properties were more than the market values of each said property. They weren't literally under the water.

However, each property had a long term tenant in it paying him rent. After paying his monthly mortgage payment, property taxes and insurance, he was still netting about $50 per property per month.

He was asking me whether or not he should sell his properties. He felt his mortgages were bad debts. Since I was still quite new in the industry at the time, I honestly didn't know what to tell him. I was trained to look for ways to maximize my clients' net worth. His three properties had negative equity so, mathematically, they were lowering his net worth calculation. I was inclined to advise him to sell his properties, but I just couldn't wrap my head around it.

What I know now, that I didn't know then, was the difference between good debt and bad debt. I didn't know about the Net Worth Myth, which I'll discuss in chapter six of the same name. Back then, I didn't know that it doesn't matter if you have negative equity in an asset as long as you have positive net cash flow. What I know now is how debt works for some and not for most.

What is the Debt Myth?

The Debt Myth is the belief that all debt is inherently bad and should be repaid as quickly as possible. It is the misguided belief that "good debt" is any debt that is attached to an appreciating asset, like a house, and "bad debt" is any debt that is attached to a depreciating asset, like a car, or any other consumer good or service. There is a lot of confusion around this. While these definitions do hold some merit, they are not quite accurate or precise enough.

In addition, The Debt Myth is the belief you must also be, and it is best to be, debt-free in order to be financially free. Obviously, there is a lot of confusion surrounding the mere definitions of "good debt" and "bad debt." We must keep in mind that we are approaching this topic from the perspective of a producer, an owner and for that matter an enlightened investor.

What is debt?

The word "debt" comes from the Latin word "debitum" meaning "something owed." I did not make up this definition. Investopedia defines debt as "An amount of money borrowed by one party from another." Most commonly, the thought of debt automatically conjures up negative connotations. People generally fear or dislike debt and thus try to avoid it at all costs. Ironically, this is a major reason why financial freedom eludes these same individuals.

Misunderstandings about debt have been taught from parent to child for generations. This ignorance is also perpetuated by the fact that many people are living lifestyles that they just can't afford. Our consumer economy revolves around selling us stuff we don't need in order to feel good about ourselves, so that we can impress people we don't even like. So, we go into debt in order to keep up.

When we think of debt, we most often think of owing money, usually to an institution, in the form of credit card debt, mortgages and car loans. These are examples of consumer debt, which is bad debt. Bad debt is painful, annoying and altogether yucky, because it's debt that we have to pay from own pockets. We have to personally trade our time in order to earn the money to pay off these debts. So, for most us, our experiences with debt are bad experiences.

Benjamin Franklin's lessons about debt

In his letter titled "Advice To A Young Tradesman From An Old One," Benjamin Franklin stated, "Credit is Money." He said, "Money is of a prolific generating Nature" and that "Money can beget Money, and its Offspring can beget more, and so on." He went on to say that for "Six Pounds a Year or about four pennies a day, a Man of [good] Credit may borrow one hundred pound" and that "the good Paymaster is Lord of another Man's Purse."

What Franklin described here is how a little bit of money and good creditworthiness can allow a borrower to have access to all the money he needs. What Franklin is referring to is using debt as leverage. As an aside, it is within this very same letter where Franklin is credited as having been the first person to coin the phrase "Time is Money." Little did people know that Franklin was trying to make the point that in order to get started, one must treat their time as if it were money. But then after one gets started, Franklin further tried to advise that it's better to have your money "beget" more money rather continue to trade your time for it.

What is the true nature of debt?

Debt is not inherently bad. Debt is not inherently good, either. To believe one or the other is like saying a hammer is good or a hammer is bad. A hammer is a hammer. It's a tool just like debt is a tool. Some people say that I'm a tool, but that's beside the point. A hammer, just like debt, can be used to build or it can be used to destroy. It can be constructive or it can be destructive.

At its essence, debt is a type of promise. The problem arises when we make promises that we don't end up delivering on. Whether we like it or not, the world as we live in it today was, and continues to be, built on debt—and credit, which is just the other side of debt. But more on credit a bit later.

If you fear all debt in general, it's because you are looking at debt from a consumer's perspective. Consumers use debt to, wait for it… consume. The cost of using debt for consumption must be repaid by the consumer long after the short-term gratification has faded away.

When we look at debt from a *producer's* perspective, debt takes on a whole new light. The income property investor uses mortgage debt to generate rental income. The business owner uses debt to finance the acquisition of a competing company increasing both market share and net cash flow. The leaders of a nation use debt to stimulate their economy.

J. Paul Getty, billionaire oil tycoon, named Fortune Magazine's richest living American in 1957, understood the concept of using debt as leverage from a producer's point of view. He borrowed hundreds of millions of dollars during his lifetime in order to extract the black liquid gold from the ground—and make his financiers, his creditors, lots and lots of money in the process.

We must learn to look at debt through the eyes of a producer. You can choose to despise debt and fall victim to it, or you can choose to embrace it and learn how to wield it for creating wealth. The choice is yours.

What is the correct definition of good debt?

A massive roadblock to accumulating financial wealth lies in our misunderstanding of what constitutes good debt and what constitutes bad debt. Ignorance and confusion over this has caused billions if not trillions of dollars to be lost by everyday people like you and me. Let's clarify these definitions once and for all.

People think that good debt is just debt that is attached to something of value. This is wrong. People also think that good debt is simply debt that is attached to something that is *growing* in value. This is also wrong. The correct definition of good debt has nothing to do with the value of what it is or isn't attached to. The correct definition of good debt and bad debt is determined by who is paying back the debt and who has control over what the debt was used to purchase in the first place—the asset.

It doesn't matter if the debt is attached to an asset that is expected to increase in value or appreciate, like your personal residence. For one thing, appreciation is speculation. There is no guarantee that your personal residence will be worth more tomorrow than it is today. We've all seen this in extreme fashion in 2008 and 2009 in the U.S. real estate market crash. Here it is: If YOU are the one paying your monthly mortgage payments then that is bad debt. It is bad debt because it is taking money out of your pocket on a regular basis.

You might be thinking "Of course, it's taking money out of my pocket. It's debt!" But, listen here, young padawan, there are ways that you can incur debt and have someone else pay it back on your behalf. Sound crazy? Crazy cool! Read on. The correct definition of "good debt" is when someone else is effectively paying back the debt for you AND putting a little extra money (positive net cash flow) into your pocket at the same time. There is no grey area with this definition. As soon as you have to take out even one penny to help service a debt, then it is no longer "good debt," but is then defined as "bad debt."

Using good debt to generate cash flow from real estate

For example, using borrowed funds, we can purchase real estate and then rent it out for a profit. The amount of rent that we charge must be enough to service our debt and any related expenses. That's called breaking even. Ideally, the rent will give us more than we need to service our debt and related expenses. That monthly surplus is called net positive cash flow. That type of debt is called good debt, because the tenant is paying the debt back for us, yet we maintain control of the thing we used the debt to purchase—the real estate.

If good debt is generating positive cash flow for us every month, then there really is no need for us to ever fully pay back that debt. Or, if our good debt is being paid down by someone else, then it makes sense for us to refinance that debt every few years and pull out some equity. We can then take that equity and use it to generate us even more cash flow by purchasing another rental property. Rinse and repeat.

Using good debt to generate cash flow in business

Here's a business example. Using borrowed funds, we can purchase something for our business that will allow us to generate more profit. Let's pretend we own a printing company and we decide to borrow money to purchase a binding and stitching machine. Instead of paying an outside company to bind and finish our books, we can bring that business in-house. This would be good debt, because the increased revenue from our existing customers will be paying back our debt for us. We own the debt. We retain control of the asset—the binding and stitching machine. We use the asset in our business to generate more revenue. In this scenario, we effectively have someone else (our clients) paying back our debt on our behalf while leaving a little extra for us every month, called profit.

Rather than take several months or years to save thousands or hundreds of thousands of dollars to buy one of these binding and stitching machines with all cash, we can use debt in a sophisticated manner that will allow us to profit today and every month going forward.

Using good debt to generate cash flow from the stock market

Very few people know that we can generate monthly cash flow from the stock market. I'm not talking about holding highly volatile stocks that yield large dividends or fixed income of 1 or 2% per year from bonds. There are actually several strategies for generating significant monthly cash flow from the stock market.

For instance, one conservative strategy is called writing covered calls wherein we can generate a very predictable 2 to 3% per month. You read that right: 2 to 3% return PER MONTH. That's 24% to 36% per year!

In a nutshell, the covered call strategy involves owning a stock and selling a short-term call option that is one or two strike prices out of the money. Now, for some of you, it may seem like I just started speaking a foreign language. This is the language of traders.

A simple way to better understand the concept of the covered call strategy is to think of your longer-term stock investment like a piece of real estate hoping that it will go up in value. Well, if you're going to hold a piece of real estate in hopes of longer term appreciation, you might as well rent it out as well and generate some monthly income, right? The same goes with your position in Apple (stock symbol: AAPL), for example. While you're holding on to AAPL, because you believe it will go up in value, you can effectively "rent out" your stocks once per month by selling people the right to buy those shares, or "call" them, away from you. This "right to buy" is a contract and this contract is known as a "call option".

In order to get into the intricate details of why and how someone would want to do a covered call, where you would find someone to buy a call option from you, the sequence of steps involved and all the "what-if scenarios" would be far beyond the scope of this book. This is what I was referring to when I said that I went out and got myself formally trained in higher level concepts of both real estate investing and financial markets trading. If you'd like a lengthier explanation of the covered call strategy and more like it, I invite you to visit CoachRoel.com/URBonuses.

In the meantime, let's say that with a little training and mentoring you were still a bit below average and were only able to earn a simple return of 1% per month using the covered call strategy. That's still 12% per year!

You don't need to use debt in order to generate monthly cash flow from the financial markets using strategies like this. However, what if you did use borrowed funds and traded using this strategy? Could you borrow at 8% per year and learn to generate 12% in annual returns? What would be your net annual return? Most would answer 4%, because a 12%

return minus 8% cost of borrowing equals 4%. In actuality, your returns would be infinite, since you didn't use any of *your* money to begin with—you borrowed your initial capital. Thus, the calculation is actually net 4% return divided by zero. If you're smartphone's calculator is truly smart, then you should get a sideways "8", which is the symbol for infinity.

The responsible thing for me to say is that investing involves risk and that investing using leverage has the potential to magnify both your losses as well as your gains. And, past performance does not guarantee future performance, bla, bla, bla. But, I'm hoping you're starting to realize that those of us that have paid the price for specialized knowledge like this are already enjoying these kinds of returns.

Consumers would rather go into debt to buy things that will take money out of their pockets. Producers go into debt to buy things that will put money INTO their pockets—like real-world financial education.

Good debt and future dollars

Another huge benefit for us is that our good debt is being repaid with future dollars. This is an interesting concept, so pay close attention. As we know by now, the purchasing power of our currencies is decreasing steadily, no matter what country we live in. A dollar's purchasing power tomorrow will be less than a dollar's purchasing power today. Couple this with the fact that whenever you borrow money, you obviously pay it back sometime in the future over a series of instalments called debt servicing. The future dollars that you use to service this debt are literally worth *less* than the dollars you originally borrowed. This is actually a very efficient way to pay back debt—with future cheaper dollars.

In the movie Austin Powers, they laughed at Dr. Evil when he demanded a huge ransom of "one *million* dollars." That's because a million dollars was actually a big deal during Dr. Evil's time in the 1960s when he was cryogenically frozen. One million dollars in 1997, after Dr. Evil was reanimated, was no longer considered a large sum. The money had decreased in value so much due to inflation that the government people could have afforded to pay Dr. Evil the one million dollars rather easily.

Imagine if the one million dollars was our debt balance. If we could defer payment for as many years as possible (like twenty-five to thirty-five years in the form of a mortgage) then we would benefit by being able to pay back our debt with cheaper, future dollars.

This strategy of borrowing money as good debt is also a very effective hedge (protection) against inflation. For all of these reasons, this is also precisely why the U.S. government printed so much money the last few years. This is why governments keep incurring debt, why they purposely devalue their currency and why they don't seem to be particularly concerned with ever paying off their debts in full. This process of printing money and devaluing their currencies also devalues their debt! Sneaky, isn't it?

Saving to invest

Good debt is also called leverage. In the hands of a skilled borrower, debt as leverage can be very powerful. Archimedes once said, "Give me a place to stand, a fulcrum and a lever long enough, and I will move the world." Used properly, debt can benefit both the lender (a.k.a. the creditor) in the form of interest paid, and it can benefit the borrower by allowing her to seize an opportunity for profit today that would otherwise not be available tomorrow.

The person that does NOT know how to use debt effectively would have no problem borrowing money in order to buy a car or pay for a vacation, yet would choose to wait until they've saved enough money over time before investing in things that could actually put more money in their pockets like rental properties, businesses, trading systems or their own financial training.

Mathematically, it is actually more cost-effective and more time-efficient to borrow money to invest than it is to save money to invest. Put another way, it's actually more expensive to save money to invest than to borrow money to invest. Think about how long it takes in months or years to save up enough money to invest. That's the lack of time-efficiency argument.

Now think about this: When we save our money to invest, we're using after-tax dollars. Most of us don't realize that when we save to invest, the cost of doing so is in the form of income taxes. On the last dollar we earn, 30% to 50% is first paid to income taxes. Then, we pay for our lifestyle—mortgage, utilities, car payments, gas, groceries and the like. If there's anything left over after that, we try to save it with the hopes that one day we'll have saved enough to put it into an investment.

We are at a humungous disadvantage when we try to invest using *after-tax* dollars. In effect, if we work to earn one gross dollar, we're in the minority if we net ten cents with which to invest. We've already lost the fight before we even step into the ring. That's like the professional boxer Manny "Pac Man" Paquiao choosing to fight Floyd "Money" Mayweather with an injured shoulder, effectively choosing to fight with one arm. No one in their right mind would do that. Oh, wait.

Borrowing to invest

On the other hand, how much income tax do we pay on borrowed money? Trick question! We don't pay any income taxes on borrowed money. How much income tax do we pay on the interest expense on borrowed money? Another trick question! We don't pay any income taxes on interest *expenses*. On the contrary, interest expenses incurred with the reasonable expectation of earning income is tax-deductible—meaning, it lowers the amount of our taxable income upon which our income taxes are calculated.

How much income tax do we pay on the income we receive from our investments? That's not a trick question, but a more difficult one to answer. Yes, we will pay income taxes on investment income, but there are ways to mitigate those taxes. Do you know the most effective way to legally pay absolutely zero income tax? Don't generate any income! Ask a silly question....

Look, there's no need to stress about how much tax we're going to pay on our investment income at this point. When we have to pay income taxes on investment income that's a good thing, because that means we've actually made some profit! Let's learn how to generate a good amount of investment income first and then we'll have the funds to hire someone to make us more tax-efficient, second.

In terms of time-efficiency, whereas it can take years to save up enough money to invest, it can take just a few days, sometimes just a few hours, to borrow the same amount of money to invest. Typically, we pay just 2 to 6% per year to borrow institutional money to invest and we can start investing almost instantaneously. It costs us 30 to 50% for us to save our own money to invest and it takes us a few years to save up enough just to get started.

What is the other side of debt?

There is another type of good debt that few people recognize. Debt is not just the owing of money. Debt is also being *owed* money. There are always two sides to debt—the borrower and the lender, the debtor and the creditor.

Provided the borrower doesn't miss a payment and eventually repays the debt in full, for the creditor (the person lending the money), debt is a good thing. This too passes the "who's paying the principal and interest test." Since the borrower is the one paying the interest, then to the creditor, this is a good use of debt.

Remember, when it comes to debt, one man's liability is another man's asset.

How can we use debt to our advantage?

To get to the next level of the economic money game, we must change the way we think about debt. There are many ways that debt can be used in a good way. Minimize, or eliminate altogether, all debts where you have to make the payments from your personal salary or wages.

Learn how to use debt as leverage in order to get money to work harder for you. Look for ways to incur debt where someone else makes the principal and interest payments on your behalf while you continue to maintain control of the asset. The asset can be a rental property, a business, a trading system or knowledge of any or all of the above. Look for ways to be the creditor.

We need to move beyond thinking that all debt is bad. We need to realize that good debt has nothing to do with the value of an asset. What makes debt good or bad depends on who is paying back that debt—you or someone else—and who retains control of the asset that the debt was used to acquire.

Myth #5:
The Retirement Myth
Freedom 85, Anyone?

> *"Be nice to your kids. They'll choose your nursing home."*
> Anonymous

I've always loved going to the Philippines. Ever since I first went back as an adult—meaning, I actually paid for my own plane ticket—in 2001, I made myself a promise to go back at least once every two years. Things didn't quite work out that way. The next time I went back was a good five years later in 2006, when I was the best man in my friends' wedding vows renewal ceremony.

Four years after that, I visited the Philippines twice in 2010—once in April and once with my girlfriend in December. By the time we got home from that December trip, she was no longer my girlfriend; she had become my fiancée. We returned to the Philippines in December 2011 to get married. Our most recent visit was in January of 2015 with our 8-month-old son. That trip lasted 3 months—a dream of mine fifteen years in the making.

I can't remember now which trip it was where I observed my retired aunts and uncles enjoying their retirement. One of my aunts owns and operates an oceanfront resort in Moal Boal, Cebu called Hale Manna Beach Resort and Coastal Gardens where that side of my family often go to for weekend getaways and definitely if we're visiting from out of the country.

I loved watching some of my older aunts and uncles (and my parents) while they played like children in the crystal clear waters where just beneath the surface lay lush multi-coloured coral and tropical fish. I watched them smiling and floating in the serene sea saying things like, "This is what retirement is all about!" as they stretched out those last two words.

One day, I observed two of my retired uncles stepping from one raft to another. Although it was a clear, sunny day the water was a bit choppy. The two rafts were moving out of unison. A moment prior, I had easily hopped from one raft to the other. The younger uncle stepped from the smaller raft to the larger raft safely, albeit with a bit of caution. Then, as I waited for the older uncle to step across, the younger uncle said "Roel. Help your tito ("tito" is Filipino for "uncle"). You're stronger!"

That's when it hit me. Two things: The first thing that hit me is I realized that my older uncle legitimately needed physical assistance doing something that I took entirely for granted just a few seconds earlier; the second thing that hit me was that the younger of my two uncles was no longer strong enough with his own footing to help the older one.

It was then that I realized that retirement, as I knew it to be up to that point, was a myth. Queue dramatic music *dun-dun-dunnnn*.

What is "The Retirement Myth"?

As a financial consultant, I had the good fortune of interviewing hundreds, if not thousands, of people about their financial goals. I learned that the *second* most popular financial goal is retirement. Not so weird, right? But I found it ironic that the most popular reason why people worked was to no longer have to work one day. Do you want to know what I found to be the *first* most popular financial goal? *Early* retirement.

The unfortunate truth is that retirement is a myth. *Traditional* retirement is a myth, that is. It is a three-fold myth that is blocking us from achieving significant wealth: Firstly, The Retirement Myth is that everyone will be able to retire at age 65. The reality is more and more people are finding it more and more difficult to retire at age 65... or age 70... or even age 75. Plus, more and more people that do retire, no matter what age, are finding themselves having to re-enter the workforce.

The second part of The Retirement Myth is almost contradictory to the first part. It's the belief that we *must* wait until age 60-plus until we can retire. The reality is we can retire whenever we want. It's just that no one—especially, not ourselves—has ever given us "permission" to retire whenever we want.

People that are willing to pay the price of early retirement don't have to wait until age 60-plus. Retiring prior to age 60 can be achieved, not in the traditional definition of retirement, but it *can* be achieved.

Thirdly, The Retirement Myth is the belief that after we retire we'll live a carefree, happy life of leisure all the way until we die. And when we do finally die, it will be sudden and in our sleep.

The reality is if you are fairly strong as you approach retirement, it's more likely that you will deteriorate slowly further on in retirement. This will most likely require a prolonged period of very expensive medically assisted care. Only the very lucky few will die peacefully and suddenly in their sleep the day after they finished climbing Mount Kilimanjaro.

What is *traditional* retirement and where did it come from?

Have you even wondered who invented retirement? Because someone had to invent it, right? Who all of a sudden woke up one day and decided that age 65 would be considered old enough to stop working and start receiving money from the government just for being old? Surely, there must have been a time *before* retirement. Can you imagine a caveman celebrating his retirement? Did elder tribesman receive a tribal pension plan or tribal social security? People didn't even live that long until fairly recently.

For much of human history, the concept of retirement didn't exist. That is, until 1883. That's when Otto Von Bismarck of Germany declared that the German government would pay a pension to its citizens starting at age 65. Can you guess how long people were living at that time? Around 45 years old. For men, it was about 46.3 years old. For women, it was about 48.3 years old. Otto was regarded as a pretty clever guy in his day.

According to the 1900 U.S. census, there were about 24 million members of the workforce, of which 1.75 million were between the ages of 10 and 15. In 1900, about 38% of the labour force worked on farms. By the end of the century, that number was less than 3%.

If you were an adult in the early 1900s, retirement wasn't much of a concern, because you were considered lucky if you lived long enough just to retire. It wasn't until 1933 that life expectancy at birth reached age 65 in the United States. Women got there first. That means the average little girl born in 1933 would've just passed away in 1998.

The Social Security Act in the U.S. was enacted in 1935 and designated 65 as the age of eligibility for Social Security benefits. The first old-age pension in Canada was introduced in 1927 for those reaching age 70. The age of eligibility for Old Age Security (OAS) benefits was changed from 70 to 65 and phased in between 1965-1969. According to the March 2012 Government of Canada Budget, in the 1970s, there were seven workers for every one person over the age of 65. At the time of the report, there were four workers per senior. The report estimated that by 2032 there would only be two workers per senior.

Between 1900 and 1999, life expectancy went from 46.3 and 48.3 years to 73.8 and 79.5 for men and women, respectively. Today, as you can imagine, people are living even longer. These days, retirement at age 65 is an achievement—something people aspire to. Retiring prior to age 65 is seen as an even greater achievement.

How has retirement changed over the years?

So, let's get this straight. Around 1900, you started work as early as age 10. You worked until age 65, provided you lived that long. You worked for 55 years and lived a handful of years in retirement, if any. You were considered lucky to live beyond age 65.

If you are a baby boomer, you probably started work around age 20. You aspire to retire before age 65. Yet, you will spend at least twice as long as your parents and grandparents in retirement.

If you are a Gen-Xer or younger, you started meaningful work closer to age 30. You aspire to retire by age 50 or even by age 40, if you're really crazy. Yet, you will live well into your 90s and maybe even into your 100s.

Way back when, people weren't too concerned with retirement. It wasn't until the 1980s that retirement started becoming a topic of interest. Since the first baby boomers reached age 60 in 2006, retirement has become a hotter topic than ever before.

We can see all too clearly the empirical evidence of victims of The Retirement Myth, with the changing demographics of the greeters at WalMart and the cashiers at McDonalds. More and more retirees have no other choice, but to return to the work force due to lack of preparedness for retirement. Worse yet, many seniors never even get to call themselves retirees. These seniors just keep on working with no end in sight requiring their government pensions to supplement their hourly wages. Hopefully, they'll remain healthy enough to finally save enough to retire one day.

The unfortunate reality of requiring care in retirement

Speaking of health, the goal of all medical research is to prolong the human life. And we're doing a pretty darn good job of it so far. People are living longer than ever before. Cost of living today is also much higher compared to average incomes than ever before. All of a sudden we've gone from almost no concern about retirement to hyper concern, over the last ten to fifteen years.

While few people like to talk about it, the concern these days isn't so much dying early and having enough life insurance to be buried. The greater concern now is living too long, paying for medical care and out-living our money!

Living longer in retirement itself would not be much of a problem if people would simply die suddenly whenever they did finally kick the bucket. But people don't generally die quickly; their bodies and minds deteriorate slowly over several years. The reality is that people are actually pretty strong and this is why we tend to die gradually.

It is very likely that many of us will require long-term care at some point. Here are some interesting numbers from Morningstar, the investment fund rating company:

- **70**: Percentage of Americans over age 65 who will need some form of long-term-care services during their lifetimes.
- **2.4 years**: Average length of stay in a long-term care facility.
- **$162,000**: Average annual costs for private-room nursing home care in Manhattan in 2011.
- **$60,000**: Average annual costs for private-room nursing home care in St. Louis in 2011.
- **21 and 17**: Average number of years, respectively, that women and men in the U.S. will be retired.
- **34**: Percentage of retirees who rely on Social Security for 90% or more of their income needs during retirement.

Why will so many people not retire at age 65?

Whether by choice or by necessity, an increasing number of people have not been retiring at age 65. There are a few, but important, non-financial reasons some people are choosing to delay retirement that are worth mentioning. Emotional well-being and physical health can be maintained and even improved by remaining active. Work also keeps people tied to broader social networks (real ones, not virtual ones) that keep people happier and gives them a reason to get out of bed each morning.

On the financial side, people are choosing to not retire by age 65 due to the high cost of health insurance in countries like the U.S. and Philippines. In Canada, where health insurance is publicly funded, we're seeing more and more services being cut. At one point, chiropractic care and eye examinations were covered by public healthcare. In several more countries, we're also seeing a trending decrease in employer-sponsored health benefits for retirees. Lower rates of traditional defined-benefit pension coverage is incentivizing people to choose to work beyond age 65.

Rather than choose early or regular retirement, more people are choosing to delay receipt of their government benefits with the goal of maximizing their social security and government pensions like the Canada Pension Plan. The amount of monthly CPP benefits you get depends solely on how much you've contributed. Plus, the government gives you a higher percentage of your regular benefit the longer you wait after age 65 to begin receiving your monthly CPP benefits.

There's a fine line between *choosing* to delay retirement and having *no choice* but to delay retirement.

The current model for retirement planning: "Save, save, save!" NOT!

The truth is, for the majority of retirees, retirement is not what you see in the T.V. commercials. The majority of would-be retirees are simply not prepared.

The current model for retirement planning is to live on less during our working years. Sacrifice and set aside as much money as possible during our healthiest and most physically capable years. Defer living the life you truly want to live for some time in the future when you can "afford" it.

The goal is to hopefully have stockpiled enough dollars by the time we decide to retire around age 65. No one knows for sure whether or not we will be able to depend on government pensions and social security when we retire. Yet, the majority of retirees today would not be able to survive without them.

From our stash of money, we're told to be careful not to spend too much on our vacations, at the casino, or buy a new car too soon. Oh, and don't get sick, don't give too much to loved ones if you choose to help them out and don't pursue any high return investments, because retirees should be happy with a "safe rate of return" (read: "low rate of return"). Hopefully, we will die before our hoard of money runs out.

It sounds like a pretty bleak scenario to me. That's because it is.

What are people doing to cope with a shitty retirement?

Victims of The Retirement Myth are forced to make do. We see them downsizing their personal residence not because they want to, but because they have to. We see them re-entering the workforce (often in retail) making it harder for younger workers to find jobs. We see them moving in with their adult children's families, because they can't even afford to rent. We also see them having no other choice but to move to another country where the savings from their home country can go much further.

That last part is not such a bad thing, because the new country tends to be somewhere warmer, like those in the Caribbean or the Philippines. But, the challenge then becomes being separated from children and grandchildren that still live in Canada, the U.S, the U.K. or Australia. A simple visit becomes quite expensive for one to see the other after a relocation.

Retirement continues to evolve

Fortunately, retirement has evolved from the beginning of the last century to the end. So too does retirement continue to evolve from the beginning of this century until now. The next evolution of retirement is where we are able to create a financially sustainable lifestyle that requires little change as we grow older, even if we end up requiring long term care.

In this seemingly utopian version of retirement, we are able to generate income from anywhere in the world as long as we have a phone connection, a laptop, tablet or smartphone, and an internet connection. Our income is non-location specific. We can just as easily work from home, from a coffee shop down the street or from the other side of the world. In this kind of retirement, since we no longer have to work a traditional 9 to 5 job, we no longer have to battle rush hour traffic nor sit in long lines at the airport in order to commute to a specific place of work.

Here, the majority of our income is on auto-pilot. We no longer have to trade our time for money. If we do trade our time for money, it's because we enjoy the work, not because our life literally depends on the income. Therefore, it's not really work for us, but a lucrative hobby that we can stop doing at any time. Best of all, this evolution of retirement can be achieved long before age 65.

Urgency or lack thereof

The icing on the cake as to why so many of us will not retire comfortably and why so many have not been able to do so is the lack of urgency. A thirty- to forty-year passive investing horizon to plan for retirement is equally to blame as any other errant factor mentioned above. This ridiculously long time horizon lulls us into a false sense of security that we always have time to get started… later.

What if we gave ourselves only five years, maximum, to start living the life of our dreams? How would that affect our plans and actions? I know it's hard to imagine, much less committing to, a five year deadline. There would be no real consequences if we failed. And therein lies my point about lack of urgency.

Retirement solutions

The ideal solution for The Retirement Myth is to first have adequate Long Term Care Insurance and amass a portfolio of income-producing assets like rental properties and online businesses and investment capital managed within a self-directed online trading account. This assumes that we are willing to invest in ourselves and our own financial education a fraction of the time and energy that we invest in our jobs and making our employers rich. Ooo! Yes, that was a definite side swipe criticizing the trading time for money mindset, in case you were wondering.

I know most of us don't like insurance of any kind. If this includes you, that's something you're going to have to get over. Financially savvy people recognize the value of insurance—especially having the types of insurance that pay us while we're still alive as opposed to only paying out loved ones after we're dead.

Long-term care insurance policies can pay us a tax-free weekly income benefit if we become physically dependent in our daily life. This regular tax-free weekly income could save us from having to sell our income-producing assets and save us from cashing in our investments. The really good long-term care insurance policies will even pay this tax-free weekly income for the rest of our life.

Income-producing assets can take many forms. Rental properties are income-producing assets. This could simply mean renting out your basement for extra income. Or, one could live in their own basement apartment and rent out the upper unit for even more rental income. This would be handy for those that plan to be snowbirds in retirement and therefore don't need a lot of space. This could also work for single people or couples with no children, even if only temporarily, just so they could receive higher monthly rental income from renting the upper unit(s).

A rental property could also simply mean having just one extra property. Imagine what having just one extra house would be like for you in retirement in addition to your personal residence. You could pay off the mortgage entirely and just sit on it collecting rent or you could learn advanced strategies to re-leverage that house (and your personal residence) to acquire additional rental properties for even more income. While paying off the mortgage entirely is not actually the best option, as I'll explain further later on, it certainly is an *easy* option.

The nice thing about rental properties, aside from monthly cash flow, is the mortgage pay-down and the potential for appreciation.

For those that are like me and suffer from a bit of wanderlust every so often, there are several ways to generate non-location specific income. You could start an online business and sell stuff on eBay. You could design your own website and sell other people's stuff. You could become a consultant and hire yourself out to large corporations which would allow you to telecommute from anywhere in the world. This is especially practical for those that have achieved a high level of intellectual skill or experience. Leveraging technology allows you to consult with your clients via long distance phone calls and web conferences over the internet.

You could also learn how to effectively manage an online trading account. I like to consider online trading as another type of online business. However, there are no competitors. It requires no marketing, no clients and no employees. Some say it's the perfect business. This is where you would trade in stocks, ETFs, options, futures or forex online using your own money. There are ways that you could effectively trade these financial instruments in order to produce a monthly income.

Do some research on low-maintenance options trading strategies like "Writing Covered Calls" as I mentioned earlier and "Credit Spreads" that can generate monthly income for you while requiring no more than an hour or two per month to maintain. My current personal favourite credit spread strategy is the Iron Condor. Sounds pretty frickin' hardcore, right? It's an options trading strategy that literally requires about half an hour of my time each month. And it doesn't matter whether the market goes up down or sideways. As long as the market stays within a (very wide) trading range, I get to keep my monthly cash flow.

I know this may sound too good to be true: "Monthly cash flow from the financial markets that isn't from dividends? Come on!" Right? But it is totally true. The knowledge exists. You just didn't know that you didn't know it exists until now.

To get into greater detail about these retirement solutions would really require a whole other book (Hey! There's an idea!). But, if you're really itching to learn more right this minute, hop on over to CoachRoel.com/URBonuses and tap into the additional free resources where I discuss some of these neat things in greater detail. And, yes, that was yet another shameless plug for my website. But that's okay, because I know there's a plethora of true value you'll find there.

Conclusion

In short, the solution for The Retirement Myth is protect the downside with insurance and learn to become an investor and/or business owner using the above principals. This doesn't take a lifetime to figure out nor achieve. With the proper education and guidance, this can certainly be attained in three to five years. If you can figure this out prior to age sixty-five, the world will be your oyster.

Myth #6:
The Net Worth Myth
Why You Don't Need To Be a Millionaire To Live Like One

Steve Jobs: "Okay, let's flip a coin."
Bill Gates: "What's a coin?"

As you know, one of the most well-known and beloved financial children's stories is "Jack and the Beanstalk." Oh, you didn't know that it was an allegory of the strained relations between the rich and the poor of its time? Well, you're in for a treat then. Here are some of the main metaphors hidden within this timeless fairy tale classic. After you absorb the wisdom in this chapter, people will no longer be able to say that you don't know Jack.

The giant in this story represents those with money and financial means—rich people, big, intimidating people—as seen by society. The giant lives in a castle, because wealthy people tend to live in big houses. Wealthy people tend to like living in places higher up than most with great views of the landscape. The giant's castle is so high up that it is actually situated in the clouds. Imagine how great that view would be.

The giant had in his possession three treasures: Gold coins; a magical goose that laid golden eggs; and, a golden harp that played beautiful music all on its own. Notice the consistent use of the gold theme.

Jack's venture into the clouds—the domain of the rich and the privileged—represents his capitalistic and entrepreneurial risk-taking to better his life. His stealing of the three treasures from the giant represents the poor man's struggle and willingness to risk life and limb to have what the wealthy have.

At first, Jack only had the courage and the foresight to steal a bag of gold coins fashioned out of the golden eggs from the magical goose that laid them. He and his no-longer-poor mother enjoyed spending these gold coins for a while *until the gold coins ran out*.

Jack and his mother running out of their ill-gotten wealth of hoarded gold coins is a metaphor for running out of one's nest egg (see the pun?). What?! But they had a massive net worth with all that gold! They should've been set for life, but yes, they eventually burned through their entire stash of gold coins. The hidden commentary here is that one cannot live for long on a finite amount of equity that is constantly being depleted to support one's lifestyle. One will eventually run out their money altogether.

Then, Jack decided to go back (to work on another entrepreneurial venture) up the bean stalk, risked his life once again to steal the goose that laid the golden eggs. This time, his entrepreneurial venture was to acquire an income-producing asset. Why? Obviously, because the goose could produce golden eggs for a long, long time and they could use those golden eggs to fund their lifestyle in perpetuity with little to no additional input of their time going forward. Sound familiar?

Why did Jack go back up the beanstalk a third time—which turned out to be his final time—when he and his mother were already financially free? Money was never really the ultimate goal. While Jack didn't need to trade his time for money anymore, ironically, he also realized that there are things that money just can't buy. He went back to steal the magical golden harp that played beautiful music all by itself. Jack wanted his once poor and over-worked mother to enjoy beautiful music in her golden years.

Wouldn't you want the same for *your* mother in retirement—financial freedom and beautiful music? That's what I want for you in your retirement... and for my mom in her retirement as well.

What is "The Net Worth Myth"?

The Net Worth Myth is the belief that you must have a high net worth in order to be financially free. People want to have a high net worth because they want to be able to buy nice things and have the free time to enjoy those things and have amazing experiences—stuff that typically costs money. They assume that in order to be able to afford these things—the stuff, the free time, the experiences—they must first have lots of money.

Well, that's certainly one way to go about it. But, as we learned from the Jack and the Bean Stalk story, sooner or later those golden eggs run out.

Zig Ziglar said, "Money won't make you happy... but everybody wants to find out for themselves." Roel Sarmago said, "Better to learn from other people's mistakes than to claim them as your own."

Why do we want to be millionaires?

Most of us don't really want lots of money just so we can spend it on material things. We don't really want lots of money just so we can provide for our family. Sure, we need *some* money to provide for our family, but you don't need to be a millionaire to provide for your family. I think deep down inside we all know that. People want to be millionaires, not for the money, but for the lifestyle that millionaires are perceived to enjoy.

The term "millionaire" is not necessarily a literal term these days, but a proverbial one. It's a short-hand to describe someone that lives a privileged lifestyle free from the constraints of a paycheque and a 9 to 5 job.

The irony is that most actual millionaires, especially in Canada, do not enjoy this kind of time freedom. That's because the majority of their net worth isn't liquid. The majority of their net worth is comprised of the equity in their personal home, the value of their personal property, their "stuff" and their retirement savings. And every dollar they withdraw from their retirement savings still has to be taxed. So, what they see in their account is definitely not what they will get to spend. Does it feel like I'm talking directly to you right now?

The proverbial millionaire has the ability to move through the world however they want, whenever they want. They have total freedom and control over their time. Thus, people want lots of money (i.e. they want to be so-called millionaires), because it gives them freedom and control over their time—how they spend it and with whom they spend it with.

If you have that kind of control over your life then you can truly say that you are wealthy. But you don't need to be an actual millionaire to have that.

What is net worth?

Again, let's make sure we're on the same page here. In accounting terms, net worth is calculated as total assets minus total liabilities. An asset is anything that has value—anything with a price tag. An asset can be home equity, vehicles, other personal property and financial assets.

Financial assets can be stocks, bonds, mutual funds, GICs (guaranteed investment certificates, in Canada), CDs (certificates of deposits) and cash.

This definition of net worth is pretty straight forward, but it is a very incomplete measure of one's financial success. You could have a multi-million dollar property with no mortgage, technically be considered a millionaire, and still lose it all if you can't afford to pay your property taxes. This would be an extreme case of being "house rich, but cash poor," a reality that many people experience today.

Why is there a Net Worth Myth in the first place?

We're told that we must reach a certain amount of net worth before we can retire. We're told we'll need a lot of money invested in order to be able to live off of the interest, dividend and capital gains income. A responsible long term projected rate of return of 4% is used by prudent financial planners these days. This 4% is supposed to manage people's expectations especially considering what happened in the 2008-2009 stock market crash. Prior to that, it was morally acceptable to use 6, 8 or even 10%.

The problem is with that tiny rate of return. If you do the math backwards, you'll find that in order for 4% of our investments to be enough for us to live off of, we will need a huge amount of investments.

Let's do the math. Let's say that pre-retirement, you and your spouse are living off of $60,000 each or $120,000 total household income. In retirement, let's say you'll receive $2000 per month each in government benefits. That's $48,000 total per year—a generous estimate. That means you'll need to make up $72,000 per year from your investments.

And on a side note, it's also a myth that people will need less money in retirement, because they're expenses will be lower. If anything, their expenses will stay exactly the same or they'll go up in retirement.

So, working backwards, $72,000 is 4% per year of $1,800,000. How many 64 year olds do you know that are on target to reach $1,800,000 in financial assets next year?

The truth about the price value of things

In reality, the dollar value of anything we have is just an opinion. That opinion only becomes reality when we decide to sell it and we have a buyer willing to buy it. Or, when we decide to pledge our stuff as collateral and someone else agrees to lend us money against it as is the case when we refinance our mortgage.

If someone offers to pay us $50 for our car and we have no other buyers in sight, then our car is only worth $50, should we choose to sell it. If we need the $50 more than we need our car, then we can only sell our car for what it's worth at that point in time. If the buyer turns around and sells it for $5000 dollars, then the car is worth that much at that point in time.

The point here is that the price value of things can fluctuate greatly depending on supply and demand and the motivation or lack of motivation of both the buyer and the seller. Just like our net worth, it's almost arbitrary and trivial to measure our net worth when we're not looking to sell something off.

Who cares if a real estate agent says your house is only worth so much if you don't plan on selling it anytime soon? Who cares if your Apple stock is worth more than it was worth last month? You'll still need a place to live and you probably wouldn't be able to live off your Apple stock proceeds if you sold it. So, why measure your net worth with anything more than a passing curiosity? Understand that your net worth number is fleeting. As we saw in 2007 to 2009, your net worth may take the stairs going up, but it most assuredly takes the elevator going down.

Why won't net worth make you financially free?

Most of us have it backwards. We hoard dollars to build up our net worth, so that we can later create cash flow by selling off our net worth slowly over time. That's fake cash flow. That's not money making money. That's called running out of money.

The answer is to focus on creating true cash flow—money making money. If you had consistent cash flow that required very little of your time and energy to maintain, then you would have no need for net worth.

Why you don't need to be a millionaire to live like one

To put this into perspective, here's another thought experiment:

Which would you choose?
- A. A net worth of $1,000,000 and cash flow of $0 per month? Or
- B. Having a net worth of $0 and cash flow of $10,000 per month?

Hopefully, it's obvious to you that option B is the best choice. That's because you'll never run out of money. If you're cash flow is non-location specific and requires little to none of your time, then you'd be able to buy nice things and have the free time to enjoy those nice things and have amazing experiences.

What should we do instead of trying to build up our net worth?

Our net worth will increase if we generate positive cash flow. Our net worth will decrease if we generate negative cash flow. For this reason, net worth growth should not be the primary goal, but the fortunate by-product of consistent positive cash flow. Especially, when we use debt as leverage and still generate positive cash flow. Then our net worth increases as our debt is paid down.

It's not "bad" to track our net worth. Nor is it bad to use net worth as a measuring stick. Just keep in mind that the pursuit of net worth is not the end all and be all of achieving financial freedom. That's the myth. Net worth is not the goal, but a progress indicator that we are simply moving in the right direction. How our net worth is being built and how our net worth is working for us to generate positive cash flow is more important than the absolute value of our net worth in and of itself.

Taking it a step further, if we can make our business and investment activities non-location specific, then we increase our ability to live a better lifestyle. Non-location specific income is not necessarily passive income. We may need to still be physically present at our computer or on the phone, but our computer and phone could be on the other side of the world. This is called telecommuting. Passive income, however, *is* a type of non-location specific income.

Learn how to generate multiple streams of income that require little to none of your time after the initial setup. Better to do the work once and get paid for the rest of your life with very little additional input of your time. Learn how to get higher returns on your money—get your money to work harder for you. Finally, learn how to keep as much of that income as possible by receiving it as tax-efficiently as possible. You won't need to generate as much cash flow if you are legally paying the least amount of taxes required on it.

Myth #7:
The Home Equity Myth
Why Paying Down Your Mortgage Faster is Bad for Your Health

> *"The dream of the older generation was to pay off a mortgage. The dream of today's young families is to get one."*
>
> Anonymous

After attending one of my financial planning seminars, back in the day, I met with a nice married couple for an initial interview, they were really obsessed with paying down their mortgage at all costs and so proud to inform me that they had almost paid off their entire mortgage. They only had about $20,000 left to go. Then I realized that they had racked up over $150,000 on their joint unsecured line of credit (LOC). Their mortgage rate at the time was 3.50%. Their LOC was 6.50%.

Every month that they couldn't or wouldn't pay off their credit cards in full with cash they would pay them off with their LOC. Effectively, they simply transferred the debt from 19.99% to 6.5%—not a bad thing. On the contrary, that isolated move is a good thing.

At the same time, any extra cash they had would be put towards their mortgage principal to the point that they neglected paying down their unsecured line of credit. They couldn't accept the fact that they had actually made no progress whatsoever. True, the total amount of liens on their house was just the $20,000 mortgage. But their $150,000 LOC was still there and it was still growing. In reality, they had a total of $170,000 worth of debt that equalled about 77% of the $220,000 property.

In the ten years that they owned that property, despite paying down their mortgage significantly, they managed to go nowhere financially overall.

What is "The Home Equity Myth"?

The Home Equity Myth is the belief that the equity in our personal residence is one of the safest places to store our wealth. It is the belief that paying down our mortgage faster is a good financial strategy, a good use of our money and a good investment.

I'm not saying that it's a bad idea to increase our home equity. This might sound confusing, because didn't I just finish saying that home equity is basically a bad place to hold our wealth? And it's a bad financial strategy to pay down our mortgage faster? This is all still true. Let me clarify: There are better ways to build up our home equity other than paying down our mortgage faster. It's good to increase our home equity; keeping it there, *hoarding* it there, however, is bad.

What is home equity?

Home equity is the difference between the value of a property and the total amount of liens registered against it. What is a lien? In law, a *lien* is a form of security interest granted over an item of property to secure the payment of a debt or performance of some other obligation. The most common form of lien that most of us will be familiar with is as a mortgage. For most people, their home equity is calculated as the difference between the value of their property and the total amount of mortgages they have on it.

Why do we pay down our mortgages faster?

Most of us aren't so much keen on building up equity in our home as we are super-keen to pay down our mortgage faster. Not so much because we want to build up our home equity, but more because we are uncomfortable with the huge debt. Since a mortgage is likely the single largest amount of debt that we will ever have in our lifetime, we will do anything and everything in our power to pay it down faster. We don't realize that a mortgage is actually the cheapest source of funds we'll ever borrow in our lifetime. That also makes it the most efficient source of borrowed funds we'll ever have access to in our lifetime.

We feel like we're doing the right thing when we pay down our mortgage faster. It gives us a false sense of security, because it feeds into our natural fear of debt. When our parents and bankers tell us we should pay down our mortgage faster, we gladly comply without contemplating the validity of the advice any further. We're told by those same people that lots of home equity is a good thing and we don't question it.

Why do we think paying down our mortgage faster is a good investment?

We don't pay attention to how much of our mortgage we've actually paid down. Most of us mistakenly believe that if we pay down our mortgage faster it helps our money to grow. We don't realize that the property value fluctuates independent of the amount of our mortgage. A house that is worth $500,000 today and worth $600,000 next year will be worth that much independent of how much or how little we tried to accelerate our mortgage payments.

Conversely, a house that is worth $500,000 today and worth $400,000 next month will lose that value no matter what the size of the mortgage is on that house. But, one thing is for sure: That homeowner just lost a whole lot of equity, if only on paper.

What is the truth about home equity?

The truth is that home equity is not a very safe place to hold our financial wealth. It is highly susceptible to fluctuations in the market. It makes us a target for identity theft. Home equity does not *work* for us, per se, and it definitely doesn't grow if we try adding to it. Home equity is equivalent to savings, but worse, because it's not liquid.

Regarding identity theft, a criminal can steal our sensitive personal information and pose as us to the bank. They can then proceed to take out a mortgage or apply for a HELOC (home equity line of credit) and withdraw the full credit limit. The only time we'd find out about this is when we start receiving collection calls or letters in the mail for non-payment. Imagine the shock of the poor unsuspecting home owner with little to no mortgage when she realizes she just had hundreds of thousands of dollars stolen from her after having slaved away to pay off that mortgage for so many years.

The truth is that hoarding our wealth in home equity is preventing our money from working for us elsewhere. Home equity is not an investment. It does nothing to attract more money to you. It's more like a sitting duck waiting to be picked off by a shotgun that is the inevitably cyclical downturn in the market. The value of your house has nothing to do with how much or how little equity you have.

Understand that home equity is only potential energy. It's like a body of water stuck behind a dam, motionless. The larger the body of water, the greater the potential energy. When that body of water is allowed to move, then it is converted into kinetic energy—energy that can be used to create.

What is the truth about paying our mortgage down faster?

This fear of mortgage debt makes no logical sense when we consider the numbers. A mortgage is the cheapest source of borrowed money we'll ever have access to. Period. As of this writing, discounted fixed rates in Canada have hovered around 2.5% to 3.0% for more than a few years. Prime lending rate for the big six major banks and almost all mortgage lenders in Canada has been lowered from 3.0% to 2.85% to 2.7% in the span of six months. When I started as a financial planner in 2004, the prime lending rate reached 6.25%. Both of those rates are still super-low when you recall that mortgage rates were double digits in the 1980s.

Consider that $100 of Canadian mortgage debt grows at roughly 3% annually. A lump sum extra mortgage payment of $100 increases your net worth by $3 after one year, since you avoided having to pay 3% on that $100 of debt. Does that make sense? Good. However, that's a very inefficient use of money.

Not only that, but the worst thing is that when our house value decreases (and it will decrease very soon) what do you think happens to all those lump sums we poured into our mortgage? That's right. It disappears. Poof! Gone. What happens to our mortgage balance when the value of our house drops? That's right. Nothing.

But, isn't it safer to pay down our mortgage ASAP?

When the value of your house goes down your mortgage balance stays the same, so the bank is undisturbed. Yet, your home equity gets chopped. So, why do the banks tell you it's "safer" to pay down your mortgage faster? By paying down your mortgage faster, you are protecting the banks from losing any of the money that they had lent to you. If you stop paying altogether, they'll simply take away your house with all that nice equity in it and sell it off to recoup their investment. It's true that paying down your mortgage faster is safer. It's just safer for the banks, *not for you*!

Really? What's the math?

So, why is paying down your mortgage faster bad for your health? Imagine for a moment how you would feel if you had a $500,000 house with a $300,000 mortgage that you've been trying to pay down aggressively for several years. You sacrificed family vacations, some creature comforts and worst of all you sacrificed investing elsewhere all in the name of paying down your mortgage faster. But you're feeling pretty good about yourself having built up $200,000-worth of home equity.

Then, the housing market takes a nose dive, not as bad as the U.S. market of 2007 to 2009, but it decreases significantly by 20%. Now, your house is worth $400,000. Your equity is down to $100,000, yet your mortgage is still $300,000! WTF?! That's 50% of your net worth gone. Poof! Just like that.

Remember, too, that when we make any payments on our mortgage it is with after-tax dollars. That means, we have already had the government take away 30 to 50% in income taxes and the after-tax crumbs we have left over are what we use to pay down our mortgage faster.

By paying down your mortgage faster you're actually putting your money at more risk, because you are exposing it to fluctuations in property values of which you have no control over and are receiving no cash flow from!

"I feel funny"

You know that yucky feeling you're feeling in your gut right now? That's called anxiety, which is caused by stress. It will be exponentially worse for your health if this scenario ever becomes your reality. Stress is bad for our health. Ergo, paying down your mortgage faster is bad for your health.

So, it doesn't make any fiscal sense whatsoever for us to pay down our mortgage any faster than we need to. Instead, we should take that extra cash and invest it in ourselves. We should learn how to make better decisions with our money, learn how to acquire income-producing assets, learn how to do no-money-down real estate deals, learn how to generate cash flow from the financial markets. No one is going to care more about our money than ourselves. Word.

How's that for a soapbox speech?

The U.S. real estate example

For those of us old enough to remember the great recession, real estate and stock market crash of 2007, 2008 and 2009, the ones that held a significant portion of their wealth in their personal homes were hardest hit. Those, however, that took out as much of their equity as possible and invested it in cash flowing investments like rental properties, were and probably are still doing fine. I know of a few such people myself. Reason being they weren't forced to sell at a loss, because their tenants continued to pay their rent. And if they had turnover, well there was no shortage of good quality tenants that were former homeowners.

Why must we stop perpetuating The Home Equity Myth?

We want to avoid being "house rich and cash poor." We want to protect ourselves from identity theft. We want to protect our wealth from a correction in the real estate market. We want to start getting the money we already have to work for us, so that we can one day stop working for money.

Two ways to force an increase in home equity

As I mentioned before, there are better ways that we can increase our home equity that are more efficient than paying down our mortgage faster:

The first way is when we purchase our property. We can force an increase in our equity by buying our property at a discount. Any amount of discount off of the fair market value of a property that we can skillfully negotiate is essentially additional equity in our pocket. This is called "making money when we buy" and it is rule number one for sophisticated real estate investors. If we are able to do this, it is still paramount that we withdraw as much of this "forced" equity as possible, as soon as possible, and use it for generating income.

The second way to increase our equity that is more efficient than paying down our mortgage faster is by forcing the appreciation of our property by increasing its use-value. There are many ways to do this ranging from cosmetic updates like painting, flooring and landscaping to renovating the kitchen and bathrooms to adding an extension or second floor. Adding an income suite is a sure fire way to increase the use-value of our property. The most effective way to increase our home equity, through forced appreciation, is to actually change the legal use(s) of our property. Changing the zoning of our property from residential to residential/commercial, for example, would dramatically increase the value of our property, thereby forcing the appreciation as well as an increase in our equity.

Spell it out for me, Roel. What should we do instead of paying down our mortgage faster and hoarding the equity in our home?

It's true that our personal mortgage is bad debt. That's because we are the ones that make the monthly payments and it's not generating us positive cash flow. But it doesn't all have to be bad debt forever. By following a good plan, our personal mortgage can be gradually morphed into good debt over time. All we need to do is take out as much equity as we can every few years and use that equity to invest in things that will produce cash flow for us.

Sample Strategy:

1. Get the lowest monthly mortgage payment. Note that I didn't say to get the lowest mortgage interest rate. You can minimize your monthly payment by spreading your payments over the longest amortization period.
2. Maintain your house in good working condition. A house in poor condition obviously has less resale value.
3. If your house is older, it is ideal to do major renovations to kitchens and bathrooms a year or two before you plan to sell, so that you can at least enjoy the improvements.
4. Use the money that you would have put towards extra mortgage payments towards investments that will generate cash flow for you. If you don't know how to acquire such cash flowing investments, then put that money towards educating yourself on how to do so. Few people pay the price to become financially free, but those that do and apply what they've learned, are living the life *you* deserve.
5. As your mortgage is naturally paid down and your house value naturally increases, refinance your mortgage and pull out as much equity as you can while maintaining the monthly payments at a sustainable level. Keeping your monthly payment low can be achieved by resetting the amortization back to the longest time period allowable.
6. Use the newly released equity for house maintenance, necessary renovations and/or acquiring additional cash flowing investments as mentioned above.

7. This same process can be applied to any and all rental property mortgages and business loans that you may have.
8. The key is to use that pent up potential wealth energy that is your home equity (and business equity) and learn how to use it to produce cash flow for you now and in perpetuity—even, and especially, when you are too old to physically work for money.

"Equity is vanity. Appreciation is speculation. Cash flow is king."
Roel Sarmago, CFP®

Bonus Myth: The Diversification Myth

How Much Do You Want to Bet I Could Stop Gambling?

> *"How do you make a small fortune in the stock market? Step 1: Start with a large fortune..."*
>
> Anonymous

Like most prudent financial planners, early on in my career, my blanket answer for growing my clients' hard earned money was to recommend they invest in a diversified portfolio of mutual funds that matched their risk tolerance. If they had a long-term time frame I'd put them in 80 to 90% equities. If they had a short-term time frame I'd put them in 80 to 90% fixed income (or bond) funds. Otherwise, I'd put them in some shade of grey in between those two extremes.

Rarely did I ever put my clients in 100% equities or 100% fixed income (or bonds). That's because, like the good little financial planner that I was, I believed in something called modern portfolio theory (MPT). Without getting too deep into the meaning of that esoteric-sounding term, MPT is basically the mutual fund version of not putting all your eggs in one basket, or what's called diversification.

But then the market began to crash in December 2007 and didn't stop crashing until March 2009. And I realized that no amount of diversification was doing anyone any good during that whole time. I started asking somewhat philosophical questions about diversification, like is diversification really the answer? And, if diversification was the answer, what was the question? Is diversification good or bad? What is true diversification anyways? *Should* I be diversified? What if I wasn't diversified? Is there a benefit to *not* being diversified? Are there any ill-effects of being diversified?

After a few years of privately questioning everything I'd been taught about diversification, I came to the conclusions that I am about to reveal to you in this chapter. I discovered the true nature of The Diversification Myth.

What is "The Diversification Myth"?

The Diversification Myth is a weird two part myth: The first part is the definition and the second part is the use of this incorrect definition of diversification as a financial strategy. First, it is the belief that being "diversified" simply means investing our money in a variety of mutual funds. The second part is the belief that this financial strategy is an effective way to protect our money as well as grow it, both at the same time.

What is diversification as most of us understand it?

According to merriam-webster.com, the word, "diversify" means "to balance (as an investment portfolio) defensively by dividing funds among securities of different industries or of different classes." Unfortunately, this is exactly what the general public's understanding is as well.

This definition technically isn't wrong. It is actually a very accurate reflection of the common understanding of the term. Diversification, in the classical sense of the word, simply means variety. But, it is precisely the execution of this definition in everyday people's lives that has done billions, if not trillions of dollars, worth of damage to our collective personal wealth. Mass misinterpretation of this term has lulled hundreds of millions of people around the world into a false sense of security. It has destroyed more wealth since the turn of this century than ever before in human history.

DIVERSIFICATION.... I think you get my point.

What is the truth about this version of diversification?

True diversification is not a matter of simply spreading your money amongst a few carefully picked mutual funds. Yes, there are a few people that have special computer programs that can construct highly efficient portfolios of mutual funds with very little overlap. I used to be one of those few people. But then I realized that even though all those eggs are in different baskets (different mutual funds), all those baskets are still on the same truck (the same stock market). Thus, they pretty much all go in the same direction whether up or down.

Newsflash: The stock market is made up of stocks, and mutual funds are made of stocks, so when the stock market goes up, that just means that the majority of the stocks within it are going... up. That's why there's a saying in the financial industry "A rising tide floats all boats."

It's true that diversification, in this sense, smooths out the ups and downs of your portfolio. But, here is a key concept that I realized and that you must understand. Smoothing out your portfolio's ups and downs may sound like a desirable thing, because it mitigates your losses on the downside. But here's the shitty part: Put another way, that also means your portfolio *will never go up as much as the overall market.*

I don't know about you, but I don't want any of my "ups" to be smoothed out at all.

The truth about stocks and bonds

Historically, stocks and bonds (a.k.a. equities and fixed income) were supposed to be negatively correlated. This means when stock prices go up, bond prices go down and vice versa. Thus, MPT states that you should have a bit of both in your portfolio. That way, when you lose money on your stocks, you make a little money on your bonds. So, overall, you end up losing less than if you only held stocks in your mutual funds. But if your stocks ever ran up, then your fixed income would always dilute those gains. That's why you'd never make as much as the overall market.

This negative correlation thing goes out the window when we have a systemic breakdown. Make note of that intelligent-sounding term. This is what we saw in 2007 to 2009 during the great recession. During that time we saw both the stock *and* the bond markets crash. They demonstrated positive correlation, not negative correlation. So, it didn't matter if you thought you had a balanced mutual fund portfolio of stocks and bonds. You still experienced a 20 to 50% decrease in your holdings.

Even if you had 100% equities with no fixed income in your mutual funds, they would never be the top five hundred (as in the S&P 500) or the top two thousand (as in the Russell 2000) stocks. The slower moving stocks would always dilute the gains of the faster moving stocks.

What is true diversification in the stock markets?

First of all, a diversified portfolio of mutual funds is pretty much an oxymoron given the fact that you can only make money when the funds go up in value over the long term. True diversification in the stock markets can only be had by active traders that know how to make money even if a stock's price goes down. True diversification in the stock markets is when you have an equal number of long trades as you have short trades. A long trade is when you make money if a stock goes up. A short trade is when you make money if a stock goes down.

Did you know that you can actually make money in the stock markets when stocks go down? Shorting a stock basically means that you sell a stock to someone today with the intention to be able to buy it from someone else at a lower price in the future. It's just like buying low and selling high, but with the sequence reversed. You sell high, first, then you buy low, second. You make your profit on the difference called the spread. This spread is also called "arbitrage." That's a nice fancy word that will make you sound smart-like: "arbitrage."

Another way that you can make money as a stock goes down is to buy "put options." The buyer of a put option is buying the right to sell 100 shares of a stock to someone at a certain price by a certain date. In other words, the buyer/owner of a put option contract has the right to "put" the 100 shares of the underlying stock to someone. The technical term for that "certain price" is called a "strike price." The term for that "certain date" is called the expiry or expiration date.

Let's illustrate this with an example. Suppose Facebook is currently trading at $94.00 per share. You can buy a single put option contract with a strike price of $95 (referred to as a "95 PUT") for $3.80 per share and it expires in about 30 days from now in September. This would then be called a "SEPT 95 PUT." But, remember that a single option contract represents 100 shares, so we have to multiply $3.80 per share by 100 shares. Thus, for an investment of $380 we can control $9400 worth of FB shares (from $94.00 per share multiplied by 100 shares). This is a nice form of leverage, where you can control a large sum of money with a relatively much smaller amount of money.

Now, let's say the very next day the price of Facebook goes from $94.00 per share down to $93.62 per share. This is good, because as a result the "SEPT 95 PUTs" are now worth $4.04 per share, or $404 for a single put option contract.

Here's the exciting part, calculating your return on investment (ROI): You invested $380 and the very next day you can sell that investment for $404 for a profit of $24. I know this doesn't sound all that exciting, but when you realize that your one day ROI is 5.94%, do you think you could get a little excited about that considering GICs and CDs return 1% to 3% PER YEAR?

Of course, this knife cuts both ways and you could have just as easily lost 5.94% or much more in one day, which is why options trading is not something you'd want to dabble in without proper training. As I touched upon in the previous chapter, few people pay the price in dollars and time and energy to learn strategies like this, but those that do and apply what they've learned, are living a pretty sweet life.

Now, you have an idea of how you can make money when a stock price goes down by shorting the stock or buying put options. You are beginning to understand that true diversification in the stock market is when you have an equal number of long (up) trades as you have short (down) trades.

That's true diversification in the stock markets which, once again, is a bit of an oxymoron the way most people try to do it. True diversification in *overall* investing—not just in the stock markets—is totally different.

What is true diversification in overall investing?

True overall diversification is investing across asset classes. There are 4 main asset classes:

- Businesses

- Real estate
- Commodities
- Paper (including stocks, bonds, mutual funds and ETFs)

True overall diversification is having a blend of these different asset classes in your portfolio. True overall diversification is also having a blend of different types of income sources:

- Employment income
- Self-employment/business income
- Rental income
- Investment income (interest, dividends and capital gains)

Even then, employment and self-employment/business income can be further broken down into location- and non-location specific sources. Examples:

- Location-specific: Traditional jobs requiring physical presence, e.g. 9-to-5 jobs
- Non-location specific: Online jobs, consulting and programming via telecommuting

What else is wrong with Diversification?

The hardest reality for me to swallow about diversification was the irony that, whether it is in business or investing, diversification is actually *not* a sound financial strategy. Billionaire investor Warren Buffett famously stated that, "Diversification is protection against ignorance," and that, "It makes little sense if you know what you're doing."

The exact opposite of diversification is actually the better financial strategy: *Specialization*

In another quote, Buffett went on to say, "You have to stick within what I call your circle of competence. You have to know what you understand and what you don't understand. It's not *terribly* important how *big* the circle is. But it's *terribly* important that you know where the *perimeter* is."
The truly successful people that we know of aren't successful because they are diversified. They are successful because they are specialized. Warren Buffet is the most successful investor the world has ever known. It wouldn't make sense for him to diversify into starting up a technology company. Mark Zuckerberg is a successful technology company co-founder and owner. It wouldn't make sense for him to diversify into real estate development.

True overall diversification is something successful people do *after* they've achieved success through specialization. Even after achieving success through specialization, they may never choose to diversify. And they'd probably do just fine.

Putting It All Together
Knowledge is Not Power

"He who hesitates is poor."
Mel Brooks

I've always loved solving problems, like riddles, brainteasers, math problems and jigsaw puzzles. When I was about six or seven years old I would put together those wood block puzzles that only contained about six to eight pieces showing a picture of a cartoon elephant or something fairly simple. As I grew older, I eventually progressed to those one-hundred- and two-hundred-piece jigsaw puzzles where the shape of each piece was almost identical to the next. The only thing different was the part of the picture it had printed on it. While any one piece could fit with any other piece, the tiny individual pictures didn't necessarily line up. This made things a lot more challenging and a lot more fun.

It was nearly impossible to complete these types of puzzles without constantly referring to the cover of the puzzle box to see what the overall picture was supposed to look like. It was through the playful learning of how to put complex jigsaw puzzles together that I first began learning the importance of the sequence of steps when solving problems.

This same methodology applies to designing our financial lives. When choosing a puzzle to solve, we first start with choosing the picture that we would most enjoy putting together representing the desired end result. The next step is to identify the puzzle pieces that form the outer edges of our picture and fit those together. Upon completion of this stage, we have a frame for our big picture. This frame is like the context within which we then proceed to work on the itty bitty details fitting the individual pieces together continuing from the outer edges gradually working our way in.

Obviously, a jigsaw puzzle, like our financial lives, can be pieced together starting with any random puzzle piece and then digging through the hundred or so other puzzle pieces to see what fits. Or, we can randomly sift through all the puzzle pieces like shuffling mah-jong tiles with the hope that we'll find two or more pieces that actually fit together. This would be the epitome of working hard, but not working smart. I think you'd agree that it would be kind of ridiculous to try to complete a two-hundred-piece jigsaw puzzle in this manner, so why do we think it makes sense to piece together our financial lives in a similar, highly inefficient, way?

Operate your financial life like a business

The purpose of any business is to generate profit. The lifeblood of every business is cash flow, no matter how profitable the business is. Businesses must continually grow in order to continue to exist, because the value of money continually decreases—the costs for supplies, labour and utilities are constantly going up because the value of money is constantly going down. The astute business owner knows that the safest way to keep the business afloat is to constantly develop new or repeat business. To purposely stand still would be a sure way to kill the business.

In order to maintain a balanced budget a business must constantly look for ways to increase cash flow, thus moving the business forward. It's like trying to stay balanced on a bike with both feet on the pedals, but remaining stationary. Sooner, rather than later, you'd fall to one side. It's easier to maintain your balance on a bike when you are pedaling and moving yourself and the bike forward.

The sustainability of a business depends on its profitability and cash flow—the movement of money as opposed to the stopping of money from moving. Just because a company is sitting on a lot of cash doesn't mean it is operating a healthy business. In September 2012, Research in Motion was sitting on over $2.2 billion in cash, but was considered to be on very shaky ground due to its declining revenues at the time. The true measure of a healthy business is positive net cash flow and consistent year-over-year growth.

Successful businesses constantly aim to improve and grow their operations. They understand that to stay alive, they must constantly grow. Ironically, maintaining the status quo doesn't maintain the status quo at all. Status quo sentences a business to dying a slow death. Successful businesses borrow money to finance expansion. They don't wait until they've saved enough cash before they decide to expand. They manage debt rather than be overly-occupied about eliminating it altogether.

Successful businesses have an inspirational vision and mission statement to guide their activities. They have long term goals broken down into manageable annual goals as well as quarterly, monthly, weekly and sometimes daily goals.

Successful businesses do spend some time engaging in research and strategizing, but they don't get stuck there for too long. They know that "A good plan violently executed now is better than a perfect plan executed next week," as General George S. Patton once said. They don't wait until they have all the answers, otherwise they'd never be able to take action. Microsoft never releases a perfect operating system. They launch, first, and then they update along the way.

The same goes for our financial lives. We can simply re-read the previous section and replace "successful businesses" with "financially successful families and individuals." Try it!

Be flexible and open to change

According to Albert Einstein, "The measure of intelligence is the ability to change." If you don't like what you're getting, change what you're doing. If you're reading this book, you have the ability to change your situation. Maybe you're already comfortable, but if you're reading this right now, it can only mean one of three things:

A. You're my mom ("Hi, Mom!"),
B. You're seriously questioning the validity of traditional (basic) financial advice in getting you to the next level, or
C. You've decided you want to ditch the traditional financial path and you're ready to do something different

If you're in category A, and you're my mom, I just want to say "Look Mom! I actually finished my book!" If you're in categories B or C, then honestly, you need a gentle kick in the pants. If I may be so blunt, get over yourself! Get your ego out of the way! Stop trying to be a know-it-all! Ironically, a sure sign of weakness (and arrogance) is assuming you don't need any help at all. The outside world will only begin to change when you change your inside world.

"[People] are eager to change their unpleasant circumstances, but unwilling to first change themselves," as James Allen so wisely observed in his 1903 classic *As a Man Thinketh*.

WHY, WHAT and HOW

Much like completing a puzzle, the most efficient way to design the life that you want is to begin with the big picture and gradually work your way down to the details. In simple terms, start with your WHY. Choose your WHAT. Then, learn HOW. This process may seem painfully obvious to some of you, but for those of you that are a little too close to the problem, I'll spell it out.

Start with your WHY: Inspiration versus Motivation

In much the same way that a business plan starts with a vision and mission statement, a personal financial plan should start with an inspirational word-picture that will serve as your ultimate guiding light, your North Star, your lighthouse in the dark of night. You will need an emotionally-charged WHY to get you through the inevitable challenges you will face along the way. As one of my mentors taught me, "If your WHY doesn't make you cry, then you need to get yourself a bigger WHY."

Don't take this step for granted. Every single human being is capable of accomplishing amazing things when given a strong enough reason—and this includes you. Merely telling yourself that you want "financial freedom" or you want to "travel more" or "help others" is not good enough—not emotionally charged enough. While you might be motivated by money, inspiration comes from something much bigger. Motivation is finite—it has to be replenished. Inspiration is infinite.

Be crazy specific. The term "financial freedom" is the most tossed around unspecific WHY that people tend to use. And yes, I know I've used it here extensively, but only for brevity. If the thought of financial freedom itself was a strong enough WHY, we'd have a lot more financially free people, but we don't. Financial freedom means different things to different people. If you truly want to live not just a better life, but the best life you could possibly create, then you're going to need to do some work articulating what that life looks like. Without it, you're like a ship without a rudder in the middle of an ocean: Helpless when a storm rolls through.

If you want to "help others," articulate who exactly you want to help or what type of "others" you want to help. Do you want to help your family? If so, which family members? Do you want to help orphans in some poor country? If so, exactly how do you want to help those orphans and in which poor country? And "how" do you want to help them? By doing what?

If you want to "travel more," decide exactly where your first travel destination will be. What country? What city? What time of year and for how long? Who would you like to travel there with? Imagine you were to sit down with a travel agent to book your dream trip. Ask yourself the same questions a travel agent would ask you.

A great way to articulate your WHY is to completely answer this question. Good questions are very powerful: "When time and money are abundant, what would I most like to do?" and proceed to describe what you would like to do when you have all the time and money in the world to do whatever you want. This is your chance to dream, so don't limit yourself. Donald Trump once said, "As long as you're going to be thinking anyway, think big." Then, re-word that WHY as if it is already your current reality and express gratitude by completing the sentence "I am so happy and grateful now that...."

A clearly defined WHY that you are extremely passionate and excited about will be your source of energy when you inevitably face challenges along the way.

Choose your WHAT

As we begin the transition away from being consumers/employees/players to becoming producers/employers/owners, we need an income-producing activity other than trading our time for money. The three main asset classes that we can choose from are real estate investing, businesses and financial markets. Commodities and paper assets can both be traded in much the same way, which is why I have put them under the umbrella of the financial markets.

Remember the name of the game is positive net cash flow that requires little to no additional input of your time once you've set up your income-producing vehicle. Actively trading the financial markets requires a high level of skill and education. For those that wish to trade the financial markets efficiently and intelligently can learn monthly cash flow strategies.

The key to mastering trading in the financial markets is leverage. Properly utilized leverage in the financial markets can actually reduce your risk dramatically and increase your probabilities of success to over 90% of achieving a 1 or 2% *monthly* return on your investment.

Real estate investing strategies like multi-family properties, commercial properties, private lending and lease option strategies afford the investor regular monthly income that may require only a few hours per month of the investor's time at most. That is, *if* the investor knows what she or he is doing.

Investing in real estate is the easiest asset class to leverage or borrow against, because it is tangible, stationary and easily protected through the use of insurance. Our entire economy is based on real estate. Even the internet requires computer servers that are housed in real estate, thus it is the world's favourite form of collateral.

Investing in businesses, either as a buyer or a founder of a business, has the most potential of all three vehicles for producing income. Businesses are also the most scalable, both up and down. This means that you can operate a very small business like online affiliate marketing and selling stuff online to much larger traditional businesses and everything in between.

Obviously, the details of the three above asset classes are beyond the scope of this book. If you would like to learn more about some of these esoteric terms, and which of these vehicles might best suit you, personally, then I invite you to register your book at CoachRoel.com/URBonuses and access some of the bonus material in the member's section. There I will be adding dedicated video tutorials of the basics of investing in each vehicle.

Once you've decided on which vehicle matches your goals and your personality the most, it would be best to focus on one vehicle at a time. Master that one vehicle, that one asset class, before attempting to learn the next asset class.

Learn HOW: Knowledge, opportunity, action

Yes, a lot of knowledge can be found for free on the internet. Perhaps all the knowledge you'll ever need is somewhere on the internet. You just have to spend hours upon hours sifting through tons of bad information in order to find the good information. Even then, it's tough to determine what information is bad and what is good. You tend to get what you paid for.

A much more time- and money-efficient alternative would be to purchase a book. Books tend to contain a logical structure within which the author's years upon years of experience are presented to the reader. Knowledge of the HOW, therefore, can be purchased. You don't need to be a hero just to have the bragging rights to say you figured it out on your own after a lifetime of trial and error, when you could've achieved the same end in a fraction of the time.

Even better than obtaining knowledge from a book is to get formally trained. There is a vast range of formal training from pre-recorded on-demand video courses to live in-person classroom-style training and everything in between. Formal training is more effective than just reading books, because it engages both the visual and auditory senses. And if the formal training involves role-playing, that's the next best thing to doing the real thing.

An even better way to learn the HOW is to utilize the expert guidance of a mentor while you do the real thing. This is the ultimate in experiential learning. Once you do the real thing successfully then that bit of experiential knowledge is yours forever.

If books alone could make you wealthy, then we'd see a much more even distribution of wealth in the world than what we see today. The ideal progression would be to utilize all of the above in this exact same sequence. First, read books. Second, get various types of formal training as you work your way up to, third, ultimately hiring a mentor to help you put all the pieces together—someone that you can ask questions to verify that what you're doing is the best course of action. Beyond that point, a coach can help you stay accountable and stay on track with what you already know you should be doing.

Once we have the knowledge, we'll be better prepared to both recognize and create opportunities where we saw no opportunities before. There are opportunities all around us that we simply can't recognize because we don't have the appropriate awareness yet.

If you've been formally trained on how to fix and flip a house, then you'd be more apt to spot a potential flip-house if you drove past it. Whereas, the uninitiated person could walk past that very same house every day and only see a dilapidated eyesore. The same goes if you've been formally trained in options trading or in business entrepreneurship.

At this point you have the specialized knowledge that enables you to recognize and create opportunities that are already sitting right under your nose. I know this next part sounds ridiculously rudimentary, but it requires mentioning nonetheless. The final piece of the HOW algorithm is "action." So important is this final step, that I have dedicated the entire next three paragraphs of this chapter to the topic of taking action.

Action, implementation, fastest-to-market are all necessary to actually begin to capitalize on the benefits of your increased knowledge and recognition of opportunities. I'm sure we all know of at least one person that we've personally met that acts like they know everything about everything, but they've done nothing with it.

Keep this in mind: If nothing changes, guess what? NOTHING CHANGES! The secret for success lies in the difference between thinking and doing. Earle Nightingale said, "We're all self-made, but only the successful ones like to admit it." Vincent Van Gogh said, "What would life be if we had no courage to attempt anything?" Michael Jackson said, "I'm starting with the man in the mirror." Enough motivational one-liners for you? How about one more? This is one of my all-time favourites: Air Canada says, "Put on your own oxygen mask before assisting others."

If knowledge alone was power, then all the librarians, college professors, PhDs and all those in academia would be the richest and most powerful people in the world. Heck, they'd be running the world. Unfortunately, this is not the case. I know of too many broke (book-) smart people. It is *applied* knowledge that is power. But, even then, application of just any knowledge is not good enough. Application of the *right* knowledge is true power. You must have the intelligence to recognize the right knowledge, have the balls to put it into action and the fortitude to follow through until you've achieved your goal.

> *"Knowledge, alone, is not power. Application of the right knowledge, consistently and passionately, is power."*
> Roel Sarmago, CFP®

The final word

So, where do we go from here? You might not like the answer. Like in the movie The Matrix, I'm offering you a choice. You can take the blue pill and choose to continue to live the illusion. The illusion is that saving your money one dollar, one pound, one euro, one peso at a time will get you to financial freedom in your lifetime. The illusion is that the equity in your home is safe and will always be there when you need it. The illusion is that one day you'll be able to retire when you're old and you'll never require medical care or have any surprise expenses and inflation will have little effect on your savings. The illusion is that everything will magically work itself out eventually by the grace of God, Allah or the Universe with no deliberate action on your part.

Or, you can take the red pill and begin to see the world (of money) as it truly is.

microphone drop

Afterword

*"If you do not change direction,
you may end up where you are heading."*
— Lao Tzu

"Would you tell me, please, which way I ought to go from here?"
"That depends a good deal on where you want to get to," said the Cat.
"I don't much care where —" said Alice.
"Then it doesn't matter which way you go," said the Cat.
"So long as I get SOMEWHERE," Alice added as an explanation.
"Oh, you're sure to do that," said the Cat,
"if you only walk long enough."
— Lewis Carroll, *Alice's Adventures in Wonderland*

Like most high school graduates, and much like Alice in her adventures in Wonderland, I didn't much care what kind of career I was working on, so long as it was a "good" one. I thought it made perfect sense that if I wanted to get a good job I should get a bachelor's degree of some sort.

I did my four years of Graphic Communications Management at Ryerson University in downtown Toronto, but I had dropped a few courses along the way (and I probably failed one or two as a result of never attending those classes). When it came to enrolling for a fifth year to finish my Bachelor of Technology degree I landed a great job in the graphic arts industry that many of my classmates would have been envious of. I postponed my theoretical education for the time being and opted for some real-world experience.

Looking back, that's when I stumbled upon my very first personal finance myth: "The Post-Secondary School Myth: The belief that a degree/diploma/certificate is a prerequisite for success." After about a year, I realized that the graphic arts industry wasn't for me. Much to my parents' chagrin, I never did go back to finish by B. Tech degree. Why, you may ask? Simple. It didn't serve me.

Applied knowledge was more my forté

Although I never did get my piece of paper (my bachelor's degree) I did realize that I had acquired some highly valuable knowledge if applied appropriately. I just knew that I didn't need a piece of paper to prove it. I decided to use my knowledge of print production and business management that I acquired in university to help launch a magazine business with a few friends of mine. I didn't need a piece of paper to be an entrepreneur.

While holding down a full-time job at a well-known alternative newsweekly called NOW Magazine, I spent nearly every other waking hour trying to keep my fledgling magazine alive. The magazine was an amazing experience, despite having never turned a profit. After a few years, we decided to accept the inevitable and lay the magazine to rest. It was a great run while it lasted.

The start of my financial *self*-education

During that time, I neglected to file my income taxes for a few years—seven years to be precise. And when I found myself in between jobs yet again I decided it was time to catch up. Because I was both a salaried employee as well as self-employed for most of those seven years, and after doing seven consecutive income tax returns, I realized that I had some influence over what the amount of my income tax bill would be each year—albeit several years after the fact.

As a sole proprietor, my income tax bill was lower in years where I had more deductions, i.e. business expenses. I learned that a lot of the things that I purchased and paid for on a regular basis were legitimate tax-deductions—things like my computer, my cell phone, some of my transportation expenses and most of my restaurant receipts—so long as they were related to my business or I was conducting business at the time.

After catching up with all of my income tax returns, I eagerly awaited seven years' worth of tax refunds. I realized that it made a lot of sense, financially-speaking, to be self-employed in some way shape or form if only part-time.

How I got started in financial planning

With impeccable timing, in the Fall of 2003, one of Canada's largest financial planning firms found my resume online and asked me to come in and interview for the position of being a financial planner. I had no idea what a financial planner was and I definitely didn't dream about being one as a kid. Remember, I was a media, publishing, borderline-artsy-fartsy kinda guy. But, when I had my interview, I was intrigued with the idea that I would become the trusted advisor for my clients and that several of my clients would eventually become my friends and vice versa.

I liked this idea. It made a lot of sense given that I often found myself informally counseling friends on their personal goals and issues anyways. Coupled with the fact that I would be self-employed, and I had just discovered that it's highly tax-efficient to be self-employed, I didn't need to be sold. The pragmatic side of me believed that it would serve me well to be a self-employed financial planner and trusted advisor on a professional level. The empathetic side of me was passionate about being able to help people. It was obvious that this would be a very good career choice for me.

I enrolled in the mutual fund licencing course and scheduled my training start date at my new career to begin six weeks later. After three weeks of studying, I realized that I had signed up for the wrong course! I only had another three weeks left with which to prepare for my exam and report for my new job. Three weeks and about a hundred-forty bucks later I passed the mutual fund licencing exam and I became a bona fide financial planner in early 2004.

Soon after that I realized that anyone in Canada (and the U.S., Philippines and most other countries) can call themselves a financial planner without any official credentials. It's not a regulated profession or title. This didn't sit well with me. So, as soon as I was on track to fulfill the minimum number of years of industry experience, I enrolled in the Certified Financial Planner course to obtain the internationally-recognized CFP® designation.

After a thousand interviews, literally

From 2004 to 2012, I estimate I must have conducted over a thousand personal financial reviews, both formal and informal. As you can imagine, I spent tens of thousands of hours discussing, analyzing and dealing with people's personal finances. After noticing more than a few patterns during these household financial interviews, the pragmatic and utilitarian side of me started asking some interesting questions.

I started questioning what the purpose of it all was—work, money, taxes and personal finances in general. I began to take special notice of what people used money for, why they wanted it, why they worked for it, how they earned it, saved it, spent it, invested it, protected it, donated it, shared it, hoarded it and often times how they were controlled by it.

I took special notice of how and why some people seemed to always have lots of money while others always seemed to have a shortage of it. I observed them and asked them question after question. I was fascinated by the differences between what this broad cross-section of people were able to manifest (or weren't able to manifest despite their efforts) when it came to money. More specifically, I paid very close attention to how they thought about money, how they respected it or didn't respect it. And, most interestingly to me, I learned about how they formed their ideas about money and who *they* learned it from.

When I first started as a financial planner, I knew almost nothing about money, except for the instructions I followed in the government booklets we used to get at the post office for completing our income tax returns. I didn't even know what a mortgage was until a few months into my new career! You have no idea how liberating it feels to finally get that off my chest.

Everything I learned about money, *I learned from being formally trained*. That is to say, almost none of what I learned about money came naturally. I also understood that most of my clients were in a very similar boat as me. The difference was that I took an interest in teaching myself about money by becoming a so-called expert in order to both help myself while at the same time helping others. And, so it was that I became passionate about sharing as much as I could about what I learned about money and personal finances. Eventually, I would take that mindset further when I sought out mentors to teach me about how the world of money *really* worked, but more on that later.

A unique vantage point

It is important to note that I am not a guru—far from it. I'm not a psychologist nor a social scientist nor a PhD in behavioural investing. My claim to fame is that, since 2004, I have had the privilege to observe and interact with a broad cross-section of the lower to upper middle class in regards to their personal finances. I have had the good fortune to work with single people still living with their parents and married couples with school-age children to retired empty nesters and multi-millionaire small business owners.

I knew more about my clients than their doctors or closest friends knew about them. Sometimes, I even knew more about individuals than their own spouse and family knew about them. I knew how my clients were doing in their job. I knew how much money they earned and how much income tax they paid every year. I knew about their health. I knew if they were planning to have children and if they were having challenges conceiving. I knew how well their kids were doing in school. I knew when their last vacation was and when and where they planned their next vacation. Sometimes, I even knew when they were planning a separation from their spouse.

To say that I was a trusted advisor is a gross understatement.

Throughout all of this discovery and privileged information, I realized that everyone's goals could basically be summed up as having the money to do whatever they wanted, whenever they wanted, with the people they loved. They wanted freedom and control over their time, how to spend it and with whom.

In case the media or other critics may want to try to label me as yet another wannabe-financial guru, I feel it's worth mentioning again to be absolutely clear. I am not a guru. Quite the contrary, I wish to never have all the answers—the enjoyment I experience from constantly learning new and higher level concepts in personal finance and investing is too fun to one day "know it all."

Enter the great recession

When the stock market began to crash in late 2007 and bottomed out in early 2009, I made it my mission to figure out why so many people were so ill-prepared for retirement. I uncovered the irony of some of the most common personal financial concepts—or *mis*-concepts, as it were—things that most people take for granted and rarely think twice about. I learned that most of the personal financial concepts that we tried to adhere to—the ones that were the most perpetuated—were actually the reasons why so few of us actually achieved our financial goals even after a lifetime of working.

I finally admitted to myself that, in large part, I was the reason why so many people were ill-prepared. As one of their most trusted advisors, I was perpetuating each and every one of the myths that I outline in this book.

Lessons learned. Solutions tested.

The fortunate result of my observations, realizations and sometimes revelations after holding my clients' hands through the Great Recession is this book. I didn't simply happen upon these discoveries all on my own. As I alluded to earlier, I started by asking questions. This led me to open my mind and my attention to other ways of thinking about money. I had become a student again. And because I was ready, my new teachers appeared.

At first, I used myself and my own family as my laboratory within which I tested these theories. Remember, I started my financial planning career in 2004. In 2012, after successfully applying the contrarian concepts outlined in this book, I was able to go into mini-retirement at the ripe old age of thirty-seven. It is now summer of 2015 as I write this.

During my three-year mini-retirement, my wife and I were able to accumulate a modest real estate investment portfolio, have our first child and spend three months living in the Philippines. During my time in the Philippines—reconnecting with cousins, aunts and uncles, and spending countless hours staring at the ocean—I felt the need to finally get this book out of me and finished. I wanted to share my discoveries and make this part of my legacy.

If you learned a few things from this book that you feel would be useful to others I ask that you give me a five-star rating on Amazon and write a positive book review there or on the website where you bought this book. This way, more people can benefit the same way that you have. It would mean so much to me.

Thank you for investing your precious time with me through this book. I hope you had as much fun reading it as I had writing it!

About The Author
"Roel was born at a very young age..."

"The more heavily a man is supposed to be taxed, the more power he has to escape being taxed."
Diogenes's First Dictum

Roel Sarmago was born in Cebu City, Philippines. His parents immigrated to Canada along with his older sister when Roel was only one year old. He currently lives in Mississauga just outside of Toronto in the province of Ontario. There, he lives with his wife and two children.

Roel's passion has always been to empower individuals with the right knowledge, tools and inspiration to take action towards achieving their dreams. Early on in his working years, Roel realized that those dreams often required money. Thus, his life's work soon evolved into helping people achieve their dreams through the most effective and efficient personal financial management strategies possible.

Roel's passions are reflected in the roles he plays as Financial Life Coach, licenced Mortgage Agent, loving husband and as "da-da" to his son and daughter. Roel is also a Property Management Consultant with Valorton Management Inc., a specialized firm that manages real estate assets for, and with, its investment partners.

Roel has been invited to speak several times at the Schulich School of Business at York University and at the University of Toronto Scarborough Campus' Investment Society and Management & Economics Students' Association due to his ability to make the seemingly dry and boring topic of personal finances almost fun and interesting. Almost.

Roel possesses the Certified Financial Planner designation - the highest designation in the financial planning industry - and has been quoted in *MoneySense Magazine* (How to prepare for a new baby. November 2011), which is ironic, since his first child was not born until April 2014.

During his tenure of over 8 years with one of Canada's largest financial planning firms, Roel was a multi-award winning Division Director. His highest achievement was ranking third amongst a peer group of over 400 Division Directors nationwide. As a result, Roel was invited to attend the President's Round Table Elite conference in Tokyo, Japan. When Roel resigned in good standing, his Division's assets under management exceeded $70 million.

A little-known fact about Roel is that he authored a study that found that "5 out of 4 adults have trouble with numbers." In this report, Roel boldly stated, "There are three kinds of people in the world: Those who can count; and, those who cannot." It is suspected that this study may be the reason why Roel did not pursue stand-up comedy beyond the amateur level, notwithstanding the fact that he stole most of his jokes from other people.

Roel is often called upon by the media for commentary on how national and global events individuals on a personal financial level. For media inquiries, visit http://www.CoachRoel.com/Media.

Roel is available for keynote speaking, group training and one-on-one financial life coaching on escaping your day job. Listen to his podcast at http://www.DayJobEscapeArtists.com where he interviews successful entrepreneurs and investors.

Bonus Resources
Total Value = $3321

Get your free instant access to the following resources, and more, here:
http://www.CoachRoel.com/URBonuses/

Mortgage-Debt Fix training video. In this video, I present a case study where I was able to help a client restructure their finances, free up over $1600 in monthly cash flow and $20,000 to renovate her basement to start home-based business. Value = $197.*

Tackle Trading is a growing online community of intelligent traders in the financial markets led by a team of seasoned coaches. This is where I get my weekly market info from an active trader's perspective. Free instant access for 90 days: Value = $447.*

3 Ways to Buy Real Estate with No Cash or Credit training video. Sound like a scam? Yeah, I thought so too at first until I got educated. Learn these three powerful concepts and start building your real estate empire today! Value = $497.*

Real Estate Connect Center, as the name implies, is a growing community of sophisticated real estate investors. Its elegance is in its simplicity: Find Money, Lend Money, Find Deals, Submit Deals. Free instant access for 30 days, plus $180 ongoing monthly discount: Value = $2180.*

*Resources subject to change without prior notice.

FREE SPECIAL REPORT
WORK LESS. MAKE MORE.
50 Part-Time Business Ideas
to Replace Your Full-Time Income

If you like the idea of *entrepreneurialism*, but don't know where to start, I invite you to read my free special report to help you get your creative juices flowing. Value = Priceless.

Get your free instant download here:
http://www.CoachRoel.com/50PartTimeBusinessIdeas

Roel's Podcast
Day Job Escape Artists

Listen to Roel interview successful entrepreneurs and investors at:
http://www.DayJobEscapeArtists.com/

Made in the USA
Middletown, DE
04 October 2016